The JOURNEY Home

90-DAY DEVOTIONAL

BY JEAN STEPHENS

The Journey Home: 90-Day Devotional

Trilogy Christian Publishers

A Wholly Owned Subsidiary of Trinity Broadcasting Network

2442 Michelle Drive

Tustin, CA 92780

Copyright © 2024 by Jean Stephens

For information, address Trilogy Christian Publishing

Rights Department, 2442 Michelle Drive, Tustin, Ca 92780.

Trilogy Christian Publishing/ TBN and colophon are trademarks of Trinity Broadcasting Network.

For information about special discounts for bulk purchases, please contact Trilogy Christian Publishing.

Trilogy Disclaimer: The views and content expressed in this book are those of the author and may not necessarily reflect the views and doctrine of Trilogy Christian Publishing or the Trinity Broadcasting Network.

10 9 8 7 6 5 4 3 2 1

Library of Congress Cataloging-in-Publication Data is available.

ISBN 979-8-89333-165-3

ISBN 979-8-89333-166-0 (ebook)

"Blessed be the Lord my Rock, Who trains my hands for war, And my fingers for battle."

Psalm 144:1 (NKJV)

Our lives are a battlefield. We get up each day and do the same thing over and over and are unaware of the warfare that really is all around us. Life is a battle. What you think, what you do, and how you respond to certain situations matter in the kingdom of God. Don't move your feet away from the battle line. *Stand*!

DEDICATION

This book is dedicated to all who have experienced the loss of someone they love. We all have experienced loss of some sort; it's part of the cycle of life. Some losses, however, are more difficult to get past than others. My heart aches for those of you who are having difficulty moving on after experiencing the loss of someone you love. May the peace and love of Jesus comfort you as you walk in the healing He has provided for you. He is there for you just waiting with open arms…run to Him. My hope and prayer is that this ninety-day journey will bring some sort of hope and peace as you encounter Him more closely.

ACKNOWLEDGMENT

To my wonderful husband, Todd Stephens, who labored with me to bring this book to life, for his love and support as we spent many hours working together with the Holy Spirit to heal the multitude of people who will read this book. (And for taking me to the beach to finish this book.)

I would also like to thank my *beautiful* volunteers who prayed me though writing this devotional. For your dedicated acts of service and financial support for the ministry. I couldn't have done it without y'all! Your love and support have been invaluable to me. May God richly bless each and every one of you!

TABLE OF CONTENTS

FOREWORD

I met Jean Stephens seven years ago in a sewing group. When I heard later she started a ministry to make bereavement gowns, I knew I wanted to be a part. You see, I am a NICU nurse, now retired, so this touched my heart deeply. Little did I know this woman would be a catalyst to change my life. During this time, I have grown in my faith and truly know the love of Jesus like never before. She has walked through difficult seasons with me and battled with me. This ministry consists of beautiful women who put on the armor of God and go into battle for each other. Make no mistake—there is a battle. Jean fights on her knees in the quiet of her prayer closet. She knows the Father, and He knows her. She walks the walk and talks the talk. She is a loud blonde who has an opinion and isn't afraid to speak her mind. She will tell you the hard things that Jesus has laid on her heart. She can make you cry and give you the best hugs ever. But make no mistake—she loves fiercely and will go to the throne for you. You may ask what qualifies her to write this book. I'll tell you—the loss of a sister, abuse, the loss of a son and then twins, three children with a severe genetic disorder, divorce, raising five boys as a single mom, a devastating illness, financial crisis.

Loss is hard; it takes your breath, shatters your heart into a million pieces, and it can prevent you from ever having joy again if you let it. Have you been there? Jean has, I have, and I'm guessing you, too, have suffered some kind of loss. A death, divorce, betrayal, prodigal child, miscarriage, still born, they all leave you broken in some way. Jean penned this book to address just that feeling. She shares stories of loss and the hope of living again with your loss. She carries the hope of healing and turning your pain into your purpose. I think you will find a calm in your storm of loss here on each page. Let the pieces of your heart be mended by the Father as you read stories of loss and prayers of healing. Repairing the heart is hard and takes work and time with the Father. I promise it's worth it. This book is God-inspired and will lead you on a journey back to life and your purpose. This is Jean's mission, and she has done it well.

She has been in the pit, at the brook of Cherith. If you don't know this story, I encourage you to read 1 Kings; it's amazing. God has sustained her and her family. A life riddled with heartache and trauma, but through it all, there was Jesus. Jean has truly been given beauty for ashes. She now has a wonderful husband who also loves the Lord—what a powerhouse they are. Jean has taught me how to fight these battles on my knees, how to keep my mouth shut (which is hard—I'm a fixer with great ideas), when to speak, and what to speak. Although I'm still a work in progress, she hasn't given up on me. When you know Jean, you know she has the true joy of the Lord. No illness, financial disaster, heartache, or anything else can take that from her. She is a Jesus lover, mother, wife, mentor, friend, teacher, and warrior.

Take this journey with her, let her teach you and love on you—you won't regret it. Seek the face of this Jesus—put your hands on His cheeks and press your forehead into His as a child would do. Let Him tell you of His everlasting, unconditional love for you. Oh, how He wants to know you. He is waiting—seek Him and let your life be forever changed. He is the One who will never leave you.

Matthew 28:20 (NKJV):

"'Teaching them to observe all that I have commanded you: and lo, I am with you always even until the end of the age.' Amen."

Kay Wilson

INTRODUCTION

This book is for mothers and fathers who have had to give their babies back to Jesus before they were able to watch them grow up. I know your pain, but most of all, He knows it very well because He had to give His Son up too. It doesn't seem to make it easier in the moment, but in time, your pain will start to heal. Trust Him through the process. He does heal the broken-hearted. Take a little time to read Isaiah 61. That is such a rich chapter of the Bible that will give you so much hope and strength for this journey. Put your hope in the One who can and will heal you if you allow Him.

DAY 1:

"If You Can"

"Jesus said to him, 'If you can'? Everything is possible for the one who believes.'"

Mark 9:23 (CSB)

This verse makes me wonder why the writer asks the question, "If you can?" Do you believe God can do what He says He can do? The day you gave your baby or your loved one to Jesus, do you believe He was with you on that horrible day? I am here to tell you He was with you and He loves you and cares for you and also your baby or loved one. He promises in His Word He will never leave or forsake you. Read Hebrews 13:5–6.

I am aware of the pain of having my baby and no crying coming from his little body as I waited, just not one sound but complete silence. It seemed like forever, but I am sure it was only a few minutes. Then to hear the dreaded words, "I am sorry; he was just too small." Oh, where was Jesus in this? How could my heart handle all this pain?

The tasks of making the funeral arrangements. Flowers? Where to bury him? What should he wear? A blanket to cover him? How can I even think of such things when I am supposed to be wrapping him in that Winnie the Pooh blanket and should be taking him home to his room all ready for him? But I will not be leaving the hospital with my bundle of joy…he will be going to a funeral home instead, and I will not see him again until we stand by the graveside and see that tiny blue casket.

I wondered what I had done to cause this to happen to my baby. I was a rebellious child, and maybe this is what God does to people who rebel against Him. I didn't take correction well, and I wasn't following the Word of God at all. Actually, I was running from Him as fast as I could, and the death of my son made me run further from him. I wanted nothing to do with a God who takes babies from their mother. What kind of God could He be?

Going home without my baby and seeing all his things made me know I wanted nothing to do with God. I was so mad at Him! Let me tell you—He is a big enough God to handle when you are mad at Him. He loved me anyway, and He kept coming after me. I saw a Bible opened in my house, and I went by and shut it as to say, "No, thank You, God." I don't need Your kind of love. You can't love me and hurt me so deeply by taking my baby!

Jesus was saying to me all along, "If I can?" Let me tell you...*He can*, and *He will*. Jesus came into this area of my life and completely healed my heart from this devastating, deep pain in my heart, not right away but in time. Do I truly understand why? No, but I trust the One who holds the whole world in His hands.

I know my son is with Jesus, and he is whole in His presence! I have no worries that one day I'll get to see my son and I'll get to still be his mother, on earth and in heaven! Heaven is real, and if you have given your life to Jesus and ask for the forgiveness of your sins, you will see your loved ones one day! There is hope on the other side of brokenness, and it is in Jesus Christ, our precious Savior! Aren't you longing for hope?

Jesus, I pray now that You help me with my unbelief. I ask You to heal all the broken areas of my heart and put me back together the way You want me to be. In Jesus' mighty name. Amen.

DAY 2:

"Fearfully and Wonderfully Made"

For you formed my inward parts; you knitted me together in my mother's womb. I praise you, for I am fearfully and wonderfully made. Wonderful are your works; my soul knows it very well. My frame was not hidden from you, when I was being made in secret, intricately woven in the depths of the earth. Your eyes saw my unformed substance; in your book were written, every one of them, the days that were formed for me, when as yet there was none of them.

Psalm 139:13–16 (ESV)

I love this verse. Jesus knew me while I was being knitted in my mother's womb! Think of this: the maker of heaven and earth has designed every little detail of your life. He loves us with an everlasting love, and He never stops pursuing us. *He loves you!* He knows your pain, and He knows your joys. He knows every little detail of your life. In fact, He wrote a book about you! Have you ever thought about that fact…He wrote a book about you!

He is the same God in both the mountains and the valleys. Life will bring both places to us; it's simply the cycle of life. We take joy on the mountaintops, but we grow in the valleys. You will likely know His presence more in the valleys than on the mountaintops. On the top of the mountain is where we experience all the good things of life…like the experience of just finding out you're going to have a baby. Oh, what a joy that day is.

It's on the mountaintop where we don't often think we need God. Everything seems to be going right, and we don't recognize our need of Him. But the valleys come when you find out that the baby you so desperately desired is going to be stillborn. Or maybe it's when you have a parent diagnosed with a terminal illness like cancer. Or maybe it's the place where you find out your spouse has been cheating on you. Or maybe it's the abortion you had in college that you just can't seem to forget. The valley is the place where the enemy haunts us. But the valley is also the place of great healing, forgiveness, growth, and restoration.

I am reminded of Psalm 30:5 (NKJV): "For His anger is but for a moment, His favor is for life; Weeping may endure for a night, But joy comes in the morning." The pain you are now feeling will begin to fade. Pain is an indicator of something wrong in us. It was never meant to be worn like a badge of honor. Pain, if held onto, will only lead to destruction. The enemy wants to keep you in a place of sorrow, pain, and heartache because when we remain in this place, our focus on Jesus is removed. Pain is part of this fleshly life we live, but we were never meant to stay in pain. We are designed to move forward toward healing and hope. And our hope is found in nothing less than Jesus' love.

If you simply are still and sit in His presence, be sure you will find Him. Remember He knows you better than anyone and He wants to spend time with you! He wants to comfort you in the deepest places of hurt in your life. He wants to be your healer! He wants to experience your joys as well as your pain. But it is *you* who must invite Him into these painful places. Are you ready to move out of that place of pain and sorrow?

Jesus, no matter my situation, I know You wanted me. I am not an orphan because I was purchased by Your blood. You placed me in my mother's womb, and I am who You say I am. Help me to remember Your great love for me. In Jesus' mighty name. Amen.

DAY 3:

"He Knows My Name"

"Listen to me, O coastlands, and give attention, you peoples from afar. The Lord called me from the womb, from the body of my mother he named my name."

Isaiah 49:1 (ESV)

Just imagine this…the God of the universe, the maker of heaven and earth, knows your name. How does that make you feel? He knows your baby's name as well. Think of this—you may have not even named your baby. But God Himself knows your child. He knew the name before you ever thought of it.

I remember after I lost my son Brandon that many well-intentioned people wouldn't even say his name for fear of offending me or not wanting to make me sad. I really think they just didn't want to hurt my feelings. But it was like people had forgotten that I had a son named Brandon. I never will forget his name, and I know that God has never forgotten him either. You see, he was Brandon in heaven before he was ever conceived.

So your baby, like Brandon, is with the Father in heaven now, even as I write this. Jesus loves children, and in fact, He tells us that we must come to Him as a child. Think of how a child comes to a parent with arms wide open, seeking that love and adoration that can only come from a loving parent. The child believes everything that comes from the parent because he/she loves and trusts Mommy or Daddy. The parent can do no wrong in the child's eyes. Father God wants us to come to Him the same way. So when you're hurting, run into the longing arms of Jesus. He is waiting for you. He knew your hurt and pain before you did…after all He bore those hurts and pain on the cross. It was not the nails that kept Jesus on the cross; it was His love for you and me!

You may never be able to bring your baby into your home with the nursery so perfectly designed and the welcome home sign hung with care. But Jesus welcomed your baby into Heaven with open arms. Your baby is waiting for you! One day when your time on this earth is done, if you have accepted Jesus as your Lord and Savior, you will be greeted by Jesus and then by your child. No matter the situation that caused their life to be cut short, they love you with an everlasting, unconditional love…just like Jesus.

If you're lucky, you will get to spend sixty or seventy years on earth with your child. But in heaven, you have all of eternity. In light of eternity, our time on this earth is but a vapor. In fact, the Bible says in

James 4:14 (I especially like it in The Passion Translation), "But you don't have a clue what tomorrow may bring. For your fleeting life is but a warm breath of air that is visible in the cold only for a moment and then vanishes!" Eternity should be your desire! But eternity requires you to give your whole life—spirit, soul, and body, heart, mind, and will—to Jesus. How will you spend your eternity?

Jesus, I am so grateful You know my name. It amazes me how much You love me. I love You, Father, and I ask You to keep me close to Your heart and heal mine as I put all my trust in You. In Jesus' name. Amen

DAY 4:

"Let the Children Come to Me"

"But Jesus said, 'Let the little children come to me and do not hinder them, for to such belongs the kingdom of heaven.'"

Matthew 19:14 (ESV)

Do you ever wonder what heaven is like? I sometimes think of my son and my twins running in heaven with access to Jesus at all times. In a commentary by David Guzik on Matthew 19, he writes, "It is marvelous that in the midst of Jesus' teaching on marriage, parents brought their children to be blessed. Today, parents should still bring their children to Jesus; He wants to bless them and welcome them into the Kingdom of Heaven." How wonderful that must be to just go sit down with Jesus and talk about anything and everything. Knowing there is no sorrow or pain there and none of the troubles of this world. It gives me great joy to know that they are well cared for by the Savior of the world!

The Scripture reminds us that all the kingdom of heaven belongs to them! The kingdom of heaven was made for our sweet children! They are safe and more alive with Him than here on this earth, and one day we will see them again! Oh, what a glorious day to see our Savior face to face and to love on our sweet children! To be able to kiss their face and hug their neck will be a dream come true, of that much I am certain.

When Jesus says in this verse, "Let the little children come to me and do not hinder them," this gives us some insight into the character of Christ. Children are great judges of character, so there must have been something in Jesus to draw the children to Him. Children must have liked Jesus a lot to willingly go to Him without prompting by a parent or any adult for that matter. Think about it—have you ever taken a child to sit on the lap of Santa Claus? They don't know this guy from Adam. Many children are afraid because they have some instinct into the character of a person and there is no trust that has been built. But with Jesus there is an internal knowing that says, "Jesus is good." They trust Him implicitly, and they love Him unconditionally.

Heaven is much more than just fluffy clouds and rainbows singing, *"Holy, holy, holy* is the Lord God Almighty." While that is certainly true, there is so much more. Heaven is sheer perfection! We cannot even think about how great it must be. I have heard people who have been taken up to heaven and described things like amusement parks, talking to animals, the best food you've ever eaten, and so much more. My mind can hardly grasp the concept of heaven, but I know it's real in the deepest recesses of my heart. Imagine spending time with the Creator of the universe and what questions you would have for Him. Being able to experience the greatest love you ever know is almost incomprehensible to me; that alone is worth a lifetime of pain, just knowing the love of God for all of eternity!

All of the kingdom of heaven is perfection. There is no pain, no hurt, no sadness, or tears. Only complete and utter joy of experiencing eternity with our Savior. And as a side benefit, we get to spend eternity with loved ones who have gone on ahead of us, provided they, too, know the Savior. Living here on this earth with so much sadness and decay, we find it really hard to understand how we can one day live in a perfect world with other perfect beings.

It is not hard to understand then that the enemy would try so desperately to prevent us from living in the place God kicked him out of. He hates God, and he hates all of God's creation. The enemy's goal is to keep us so paralyzed that we are unable to walk out God's calling on our life. The enemy doesn't want us to experience the things he willingly gave up. He is forever cursed, and one day he will be condemned forever to the pits of hell. Hell was created for Satan, not for us. We have a choice between heaven and hell. We can choose to spend eternity in eternal torment, or we can choose to spend eternity in a place where there is no imperfection. How will you choose to spend eternity?

Yeshua, may I always come to You with the heart of a little child. With the awe and wonder of Your majesty, Your glory, and Your power. Oh, how I long to sit with You and let You just hold me. I confess I need You. Come heal my heart and sit with me. In the mighty name of our Lord Yeshua. Amen.

DAY 5:

"Seasons Under Heaven"

For everything there is a season, and a time for every matter under heaven: a time to be born, and a time to die; a time to plant, and a time to pluck up what is planted; a time to kill, and a time to heal; a time to break down, and a time to build up; a time to weep, and a time to laugh; a time to mourn, and a time to dance; a time to cast away stones, and a time to gather stones together; a time to embrace, and a time to refrain from embracing; a time to seek, and a time to lose; a time to keep, and a time to cast away; a time to tear, and a time to sew; a time to keep silence, and a time to speak; a time to love, and a time to hate; a time for war, and a time for peace.

Ecclesiastes 3:1–8 (ESV)

As you read these verses, what comes to mind? As the scripture says, there is a season for everything.

Seasons of mourning serve a good purpose—they remind us of our need to put our faith and hope in God. God gives us one opportunity—this life on earth—to know Him and receive His gift of salvation. If we live only to party and have fun, we will be ill-prepared for eternity.[1]

Seasons are a necessary part of life. I would say it is the cycle of life. We all have seasons of mourning in our life; mourning is an inevitable part of life, just like spring and summer, winter and fall. However, as believers we mourn differently than unbelievers. A believer mourns as if in winter when things die off awaiting spring when new life begins. We sorrow over the death, but we have the hope of being resurrected anew. For an unbeliever, they can get stuck in a winter season after a death of a loved one or after a loss of something important in their life. It can seem cold and hopeless. The hope of ever seeing a loved one again someday is nowhere to be found in the life of an unbeliever.

God is with us in every season of our life. When we face the unknown, we can trust that He is in control and working out every situation for our good. Psalms chapter 1 teaches us that by putting our delight in studying the ways of the Lord that we will be like a tree rooted by a stream that produces good fruit.[2]

---

1 "What Does It Mean That There Is a Time to Mourn and a Time to Dance (Ecclesiastes 3:4)?" Got Questions, last updated January 17, 2022, https://www.gotquestions.org/time-to-mourn-and-time-to-dance.html.

2 "3 Bible Verses for Seasons of Change," Bethesda Senior Living, posted October 9, 2018, https://www.bethesdaseniorliving.com/blog/3-bible-verses-for-seasons-of-change.

Time and seasons can be relative to us depending on where we are at in our walk of life. For example, when you are young, time seems to last forever. We are constantly looking for the next season of life. As a child I know I was excited to turn ten years old, and as soon as I did, my next target was thirteen, then sixteen, then eighteen, then twenty-one…well, you get the idea. We are constantly looking to milestones in our lives.

There comes a time when we realize that our time here on earth is a short season. When we are young, we think we will live forever. With time we begin to understand that life is short and we will not live as we know it forever. The older we get, the faster our seasons of life seem to pass by us. We are no longer looking for the next milestone. Some of us are simply looking to get through to the next day. We begin to see people we love and care about pass on into eternity. This alone gives us a different perspective on life and causes us to be more reflective on our own life. We begin to change in many ways as we mature in life and as we learn to come to the end of ourselves. This is true of our walk in Christ as well. Jesus, as our example and prototype, leads us to a place of peace and a consistency in our walk with Him. We are no longer swayed by the cares and worries of this world. Our focus shifts from the temporal aspects of this world to the eternal aspects of heaven.

"We all experience change and transition in life. Sometimes life is exciting, dynamic, and we feel on top of the world. At other times we just want to go away and escape the situation—as King David said, 'Oh that I could fly away with wings like a dove.'"[3]

We must understand the seasons. If we do not understand that there are seasons in life, we may draw the wrong conclusions about what is happening in our lives or the reasons for it. God has a plan and a purpose to make your life beautiful.

It's important to note that God is in every season of our life, and we need to remember that no season lasts forever. If you are stuck in a season, maybe you should take a reflective look at why you haven't progressed into the next season. Ask God why you seem to be stuck. Perhaps you have failed to do the last thing He has asked you to do, or maybe you are stuck in a season of mourning.

We can be confident that God is working things out for our good no matter how things are going in our external world. God's main purpose is to prepare and form us for eternity, to conform us to the image of Jesus Christ.

> *When we understand that, we can understand that we are not going to have easy seasons all the time. Even the blessed man of Psalm 1 who meditates on the world bears fruit "in its season" (Ps 1:1–3). Whether we see fruit in our current season or not, God is still at work, preparing something good for us.[4]*

---

3 Larry Kreider, "Never Forget This Truth," posted August 8, 2018, https://dcfi.org/2018/08/never-forget-this-truth/.
4 "Every Season Brings Its Joy Meaning," Lux Seattle, posted January 8, 2021, https://luxseattle.com/194tr/every-season-brings-its-joy-meaning-34b27f.

What season are you in?

Lord, as the seasons change, I ask You to change me. Change my way of thinking and how I receive Your Word in my life. Heal my mind, body, and soul and lead me closer to You. In Jesus' name. Amen.

DAY 6:

"This Child I Prayed For"

" 'For this child I prayed, and the Lord has granted me my request which I asked of Him. Therefore I have also dedicated him to the Lord; as long as he lives he is dedicated to the Lord.' And they worshiped the Lord there."

1 Samuel 1:27–28 (AMP)

As you read this book, many of you have prayed and prayed for a baby. When you finally get word that you are pregnant, you become so excited and are filled with anticipation. Hope springs eternal and new life has begun.

For those who have experienced the loss of a baby, the hope can quickly turn to sadness and despair. It might even seem as soon as God answered the prayer to get pregnant, the hope of a baby was dashed to pieces when no baby came home. It can be hard to take comfort from anything or anyone at this time. Some of you have prayed and prayed for a child only to never get pregnant at all. You may be wondering why you even picked this book up. Then you begin reading and find yourself here on day 6. You may find yourself saying, "I've prayed until I can't pray anymore for a baby, but God doesn't hear me."

There may be a variety of answers to the situations above. But sometimes there may be no answer at all. I know this may not bring you comfort right now. But know this…God does love you, and He has not forgotten you! We may feel like we are being disciplined for something we have done before we came to Christ or because we haven't come to Him at all. You may feel as though God doesn't hear you, so you stop praying entirely. It's only in His presence that you will know truth.

Many of you may identify with the story of Hannah and Samuel found in the book of First Samuel. Only to finally be granted a child, yet to have to give that child up before you are ready. But have you ever thought that maybe God created you to be a superhero to an unwanted child who was born into a difficult situation? You could be that child's answer to prayer. God rarely answers prayers the way we think He should. But God's answers are always right, and His plans are for our good. So don't be too quick to blame God when your plans don't line up with His. Most of the time, we must align our life and our lifestyle to God's perfect design.

You have not been created by mistake! God doesn't make mistakes…we do. God will take our mess and make a message out of it. We must submit to His will and let go of all the things we think are important. For some of us we need to hold on loosely to what we've already been given. Life has a way of coming at us fast and unexpectedly. The reality is there are few absolutes in this life; the most important absolute truth is this…God is good, and He loves you with an everlasting love. You are never beyond His reach. Your hopes and dreams may not look like His plans for your life, and we are not guaranteed anything. Remember this: God is for you, and He is not against you.

For some of you, there is the hope of a rainbow baby, a child born after the loss of another baby. For others, you may get to choose your baby through adoption. Just don't give up hope if your prayers aren't answered the way you think they should be answered. Remember, Hannah was blessed with a baby after many years of infertility. But she also vowed to dedicate that child to the Lord's service, so her time with Samuel was cut short. Few, if any, of us get our prayers answered in our time or in our way. I know it hasn't worked that way for me. There have been many trials and much travailing in prayer. But through it all I know God is good all the time! Can you, too, say that God is good all the time?

Sweet, sweet Jesus, I prayed and prayed for this child, and You took them home to live with You before I even got to know them. Help me, Jesus, to not try to understand Your ways but accept them and be able to go on and live and fulfill my purpose on this earth. I need Your strength to do all You have for me to do and to be able to carry out my assignment and to trust You. In Jesus' name. Amen.

DAY 7:

"My Redeemer Lives"

"For I know that my Redeemer lives, and at the last he will stand upon the earth. And after my skin has been thus destroyed, yet in my flesh I shall see God."

Job 19:25–26 (ESV)

The Hebrew word for Redeemer is *goel* (pronounced *guy al*); it is closely related to being the next of kin or a kinsmen redeemer. It's meant to say a deliverance from sin or captivity, biblically speaking. In Hebrew, it's a person who, as the nearest relative of someone, is charged with the duty of restoring that person's rights and avenging wrongs done to him or her. One duty of the *goel* was to redeem (purchase back) a relative who had been sold into slavery. Another was to avenge the death of a relative who had been wrongly killed—one carrying out this vengeance.

In this instance in Job, it is believed that Job looked at God Himself as his redeemer. This fits really well with us as well. No matter how you look at it, as God as your kinsman redeemer who is to save you from captivity or as the God who avenges you, this passage of Scripture is filled with hope. Job could have easily blamed God for his predicament, but he chose to look ahead to the redemption found in God.

Think of it—after your days are done and God calls you home, you *will* see Him face to face. God is your redeemer! He sent His one and only Son (John 3:16) to lift us up out of the muck and the mire to put us on a firm foundation. He is our vindicator against all of Satan's accusations against us.

Jesus is standing in the courtroom of heaven waiting to defend you from all that Satan accuses you. All your sins and all of your pain were atoned for by just one drop of His blood.

Can you imagine being in Job's position? He lost everything, his wealth, his health, and all his family, except for his wife. You may feel like Job at times, especially after losing a child. Could you maintain your faith like Job did? Or do you blame God for your loss? Job is a great example for us on how to react in times of trouble. Make no mistake—Job wasn't perfect, but he did come back to his faith in God. He stood firm in the face of accusation and opposition. Job didn't deserve the losses he incurred, and likely you don't deserve the losses you have incurred. Stand firm in faith and hold onto the hope that rests in Him.

Remember there are no guarantees in this life. We live in a sinful world that He gave us dominion over. He gave us legal rights to mess it all up. We have certainly found a way to make things ugly in our life sometimes. But God is faithful, and He has purchased, at a very high price, our redemption. Jesus made a way when there was no other way. Job was blessed for his faithfulness with double what he had before his trials. Does that mean you will experience increase? Not necessarily, but it sure does give us hope if we keep our eyes on Him. We cannot put our focus on fleshly desires. But when we abide in Him, He will bless us abundantly with more than we could ask or imagine.

We must put first things first. Or major on the majors. It's all about our focus. So where's your focus? Is it on God and His faithfulness, or are you focused on the things of this earth?

Father God, I pray for all those reading this that have experienced the loss of a loved one. That they may feel your redemptive powers right now as they read this. I pray their focus would be on sitting at the feet of the Savior and Your faithfulness in their life. Let them not dwell on the things of this earth, but let them experience your goodness. In Jesus' name.

Amen!

DAY 8:

"I Will Trust in You"

"And we know that all things work together for good to those who love God, to those who are the called according to His purpose."

Romans 8:28 (NKJV)

The primary reference of all things is the sufferings of this present time. There is an immense amount of comfort from this verse. It is my go-to verse when life hands me a curve ball. Whether it is a disappointment, a setback, or a wound, sometimes there are things that happen to us in this life that we just don't understand. In the moment, we can't seem to find a way out or even some sort of silver lining in the dark cloud in which we are surrounded.

Let's face it—none of us have it all together and have a contingency plan for every situation we may encounter in life. We are prone to be concerned, worried, or upset until something sets us back on the right track. For me, this verse is the course correction I need when I get into a funk over some unexpected event. There are many things that happen to us that we won't understand, no matter how hard we try to avoid these things. You're not always going to understand the circumstances.

When we come against these things in life that set us back, it is important to have a firm foundation where we do have a solid understanding. For me, the firm foundation begins with God's unconditional love for me. His love for me is confirmed by the Father sending His one and only Son to die for my sins (see John 3:16). I *know God's* ways are not my ways and His thoughts are not my thoughts (see Isaiah 55:8–9). These are foundational, absolute truths in my life. How do I know this? The Bible tells me so… that is how I know.

God is in control of the circumstances of my life. He doesn't always create the things that happen to us, but He will allow them to happen to us. But I do know this—if God allowed something to happen to me, it will always work out for my good. In my opinion, this is one of those things that you can only see from the other side of brokenness. When the pain is softened, we can look back and see how God orchestrated events for our own well-being. Rarely will you notice this when you are in the midst of the storm.

We must always come back to our own foundational truths during the storms. Our lives may be shaken, but we have that firm foundation upon which we can rely. God and His Word are your firm foundation…this is where we must put our trust. He alone is worthy of all our trust. He is the solid rock upon which I stand! But the firm foundation can only be built through a close, intimate relationship that is built in the dark. In your secret place, you will find Him.

When I think of the firm foundation and how it is built, I think of the Shema…this is the centerpiece of the Jewish prayers in the morning and the evening prayer time. It starts with the words found in Deuteronomy 6:4–5 (NKJV), "Hear, O Israel: The Lord our God, the Lord is one! You shall love the Lord your God with all your heart, with all your soul, and with all your strength."

This perfectly illustrates why He is our firm foundation. His love for us and our love for Him constitute an unshakeable foundation that will stand strong in the face of all adversity.

I have built my life on the foundation of God and His Word; His faithfulness and mercies are new every day. Isn't that comforting? The question is: What kind of foundation are we relying on? A financial foundation won't sustain you. Friends and family won't sustain you. Your work won't sustain you. There's only one foundation you can rely on. What foundation have you built your life upon?

Father God, I choose to put my trust in You. I ask You to come to me and heal these areas in my heart that are so broken that I can hardly breathe. I confess I need You right here and right now. Help me, Lord, to trust You when I can't understand my situation. In Jesus' name.

Amen.

DAY 9:

"Make Me Broken"

"He heals the brokenhearted And binds up their wounds."

Psalm 147:3 (NKJV)

This is a verse after losing a baby or a child that you have to stay in prayer to understand. The wounds of the loss are so raw, and your heart is so shattered that you think to yourself, *How can He heal this?* I have some good news for you…He can, and He will if you hand it over to Him.

During times of loss, many of us will internalize the pain and put on a brave face for all the world to see, but when we are alone with our thoughts, the wounds have a way of binding us up as if being put in a straight jacket. We are fully intact. We just aren't functional. What we need is to be freed from the ties that bind us.

Our freedom is assaulted by the enemy every single day, especially in this day and age. We have people telling us how to think. We have people telling us, "Do this, but don't do that." We have governments that tell us what we can and cannot say even though we have a constitution in the United States to protect our freedoms and God-given rights.

Freedom…is a word that brings a variety of thoughts to people. To some who live in countries where freedom is bound, freedom is desired more than anything. But to those in the United States, in this day and age, freedom is taken for granted. Freedom in the United States is being assaulted, but there is a freedom that will stand for eternity.

That kind of freedom is freedom that only comes through our Lord and Savior, Jesus Christ. It was prophesied by the prophet Isaiah some 700 years before His birth.

"The Spirit of the Lord God is upon Me, Because the Lord has anointed Me To preach good tidings to the poor; He has sent Me to heal the brokenhearted, To proclaim liberty to the captives, And the opening of the prison to those who are bound" (Isaiah 61:1, NKJV).

Freedom from the captivity of sin and eternal judgment is what Isaiah was proclaiming. This is confirmed in the book of 2 Corinthians.

"Now the Lord is the Spirit, and where the Spirit of the Lord is, there is freedom" (2 Corinthians 3:17, NIV).

Through these two verses alone, it is abundantly clear that true freedom only comes from the Lord, Jesus Christ.

While we in the US have a constitution that protects our freedoms, it is an imitation of our freedom in Christ. Get free from the bondage, the hurt, and the wounds. Let go and let God; He will heal everything in you!

So strive for true freedom, my friends! If you are a believer, then you have true freedom that can never be taken from you because of the blood covenant we have in Jesus Christ! He will bind the wounds and heal you from all brokenness, mending you back together one stitch at a time. He will heal your wounds and break the chains that bind you. Isn't this the kind of freedom we all desire?

Jesus, I am so broken, and I know only You can fix me. Take all this pain and turn it into Your glory and purpose for my life. Help me lean into You and clear my heart, mind, and soul of all the pollution of this world. I love You, Jesus! I know You love me enough that You died for me. In Jesus' name. Amen.

DAY 10:

"The Hope of the Beloved"

Beloved brothers and sisters, we want you to be quite certain about the truth concerning those who have passed away, so that you won't be overwhelmed with grief like many others who have no hope. For if we believe that Jesus died and rose again, we also believe that God will bring with Jesus those who died while believing in him.

1 Thessalonians 4:13–14 (TPT)

Beloved…that is an interesting word. It means to be wholly and affectionately loved by the Father. Specifically, the woman is the Master's finishing touch. She is the crown of creation. Upon creating Adam, God noted that His work was incomplete. As it says in Genesis chapter 2, verse 22 (NKJV), "Then the rib which the Lord God had taken from man He made into a woman, and He brought her to the man." As cliché as it sounds, the woman made the man a completed work.

From the man and woman comes their own creation. That was by God's design. When we have a child, we are doing the Master's work… We are creating with the help of God, of course. That is part of the joy of giving birth…"bone of my bone, flesh of my flesh." The baby is the intermingling of two distinct DNA chains. Literally the mixing of the characteristics of two individuals. The beauty of this event is unmistakable.

I believe this is partially why it is so painful when we lose a child at birth or shortly thereafter. We literally are losing a part of ourselves. It is devastating to lose a child at any age, but I think it is especially painful to lose one just as their life is beginning. The hope and expectations from finding out you are pregnant quickly die along with the baby if you are not careful.

We are given the hope of spending eternity with our loved ones as it is stated in our featured verse for today: 1 Thessalonians 4:13–14. These verses clearly demonstrate that as long as we maintain our belief in Jesus Christ. In the end, Jesus is bringing with Him those of have gone ahead of us who believed in Jesus. A baby makes it into the kingdom because they have not experienced the sinfulness of this world. They are innocent because they are incapable of making a decision that would stand for eternity. There is beauty that comes out of the darkness. What the devil intends for evil, God will use for our good.

Our part to play when our child goes to heaven is to maintain our belief in Jesus and to produce good fruit in our lives. We must finish our race well! There come forks in the road for us as Christians where we must decide the path we follow. We can take the path that leads to Christ, or we can follow the fleshly path that leads to destruction. Unfortunately, many times these forks in the road come when we lose someone close to us. Making that right choice will mature us in our walk with Jesus. These moments of decision are milestones that will lead us closer to Him.

Once we carefully mature in Christ, we produce glory for His kingdom, and when God speaks, know that He will never contradict His Word, so make sure that the voice you hear lines up with the Word you read. The principles of His Word will give you the strength you need to trust His heart even though you can't see His face.

I would ask you today…are you in the Word daily? Do you know His voice? Are you being obedient? We have so much to do for the kingdom. I can only hope that I will be like Paul and finish my race well.

"I have fought the good fight, I have finished the race, I have kept the faith. Finally, there is laid up for me the crown of righteousness, which the Lord, the righteous Judge, will give to me on that Day, and not to me only but also to all who have loved His appearing" (2 Timothy 4:7–8, NKJV). The day I see Him face to face will be a day I have longed for my entire life. I can only imagine dancing with Jesus and spending eternity with Him and my child! So today I would ask you…do you know Him?

Jesus, thank You for Your hope. I will cling to it like I am clinging to You. Give me Your hope in my situation that I will laugh again and find joy, even if it's only in the moment. Lord, You are my only hope. I love You. In Jesus' name. Amen.

DAY 11:

"Shalom"

"I leave the gift of peace with you—my peace. Not the kind of fragile peace given by the world, but my perfect peace. Don't yield to fear or be troubled in your hearts—instead, be courageous!"

John 14:27 (TPT)

Finding peace during the death of a loved one is very hard. Leaving the hospital without the baby you were to bring home is just heart-wrenching. Even while in the hospital, you feel segregated from all the other families. You feel like you are the only one leaving the hospital without your baby. That may or may not be true. But what is true is that you feel completely alone. You may even feel a separation from your husband or other loved one. Your body is still responding as if the baby was there and fully alive. But there is no peace, and there is no life…at least so it seems.

We are immediately tasked with making funeral arrangements and decisions a parent never thought they would have to make. It becomes so overwhelming that it's difficult to find any form of hope or peace. It's in these moments where fear comes in or resentment or anger and certainly you are flooded with sadness. While well-meaning people say all kinds of things to try to make you feel better, they can't feel what you feel unless they, too, have experienced this great loss. Many times, when we face problems, we attribute our troubles to God. But this is because we have set up idols in our heart…idols of pride and intellect. So we must get rid of the idols in our heart and allow Jesus to guide us.

It's as if you are surrounded in utter darkness. You're so afraid to take a step because you have no idea where that step will lead you. This is where faith comes in…you may not know what direction to go or even have the ability to make any decision whatsoever. It's during this time we must put all our trust in God. Our faith may be weak at first, but with every seemingly blind step we take, our faith will grow stronger and stronger. Thus, faith must become a way of life or a path we choose to live.

God did not cause this tragedy to come upon you! This is a truth you must know deep in your heart. You may need to tell yourself moment by moment every time the enemy says to you, "See what your God did to you?" You tell him, "*No*, my God loves me and wants only the best for me, and He works *all things* together for my good and for His glory because I love Him."

The enemy is a liar and the father of all lies (see John 8:44), and he seeks to destroy you and separate you from God. Have you ever told God, "I trust You even if my situation never changes"? Even if I never bring a baby home, I trust that You are a good, good Father and that Your ways are not my ways. I trust You no matter what! What the enemy meant for harm, God intends for good. Every test is sent to perfect our character.

This is where we gain our peace…having our faith placed completely in Him. And it's not like it's any old peace; it's the perfect peace, shalom, that the Jewish faith describes as nothing broken, nothing missing. Allow this to envelope you during this time…His shalom, His perfect peace!

Ask yourself, *How can I allow what has happened to me to transform me to look more like Jesus?*

Yeshua, I am trying to find peace in my situation. I need Your help. I see all the darkness around, and I can't seem to find Your light. Lead me into Your perfect peace. In Jesus' name.
Amen.

DAY 12:

"Even When It Hurts I Will Trust You"

"He will wipe away every tear from their eyes and eliminate death entirely. No one will mourn or weep any longer. The pain of wounds will no longer exist, for the old order has ceased." And God-Enthroned spoke to me and said, "Consider this! I am making everything to be new and fresh. Write down at once all that I have told you, because each word is trustworthy and dependable."

Revelation 21:4–5 (TPT)

This is not your fault. Our ministry has encountered many women who blame themselves for the loss of their baby. So let me say it again…this is not your fault. These women blame themselves for not eating right or not doing this, or they should have stopped doing that. It almost sounds silly when you think about this issue with a commonsense mindset. But commonsense gets thrown right out the window when it comes to losing your child at birth. There is no explanation for the death of a baby that makes any sense at all, especially to the expectant mother.

The cause of death becomes unimportant during this time. There's only one thing a mother knows— she will not be going home with her baby. The mother only experiences pain and grief. The hope of new life fades into the reality of death. The cycle of mourning and grief begins. Soon anger creeps in, and so does the desire to place blame somewhere, anywhere, whether it makes sense or not. Often a mother will blame herself. But what happens when blame cannot be assigned or when there is no explanation? Can you forgive yourself? What about the person you assigned blame to? Can you forgive them?

Forgiveness is a vital part of our Christian walk. It is a command of God. Forgiveness is not optional, even if the person you must forgive is you. Forgiving yourself is one of the most difficult things to do…we are our own worst critics. We must remember that through Jesus Christ God forgave us and gave Himself up for our sins. His grace is enough. So how can we put ourselves in a position that nullifies His forgiveness for us? Are we better than God, who says we are forgiven? Do we place ourselves in a position of higher authority than God? When we refuse to forgive ourselves or others, we are placing ourselves in the throne of God. This is a vital subject for the Christian and a subject we really must master. There are 127 verses in the Bible that talk about forgiving. Even the apostles struggled with forgiveness as evidenced by Peter questioning Jesus on how many times we are to forgive someone who has wronged us (see Matthew 18:21). Peter said, "Do I forgive up to seven times?" Jesus looked at Peter and said, "Not seven times but seventy times seven." What Jesus meant by this was that you are to forgive as many times as it takes.

How do you know you have forgiven someone or even yourself? You might have to forgive over and over and over. You might have to forgive moment by moment. You might have to forgive daily. You will need to forgive until you can think about the situation or the person, and it no longer has the effect of anger, sadness, or bitterness connected to it. You may even get to the point where you have forgiven so much that you begin to develop godly sorrow over the person or situation, where you genuinely feel sorry for the person, and you have truly let go of the offense and have given it over to God.

There is coming a day when there will be no offense, no sadness, no heartache, no pain. There will be no need for mourning or sorrow or weeping. One day when you enter through the gates of heaven, nothing on this earth will matter any longer. But in order to arrive at the pearly gates of heaven and to enter in, one must let go of any offense that they are holding against anyone. Forgiveness is not optional; it is commanded. Do you truly understand God's forgiveness?

Jesus, help me forgive anyone who has harmed me and then help me forgive myself. I need
Your help because I can't do it on my own. In Jesus' name. Amen.

DAY 13:

"Have Your Way, My King"

"Though he brings grief, he will show compassion, so great is his unfailing love."

Lamentations 3:32 (NIV)

We've discussed many different types of loss already. But what about the loss of a child while they are still alive? I am referring to the prodigal child. This is the child that gets offended or believes they know more than the parent or the one who chooses a reckless lifestyle. Whatever the reason for the prodigal to leave home, the loss of this child can be very painful. A mom and dad never really stop worrying about their child even when they are completely grown. In some cases, these children completely cut off all communication. The unknown is almost worse than knowing what is going on with your prodigal. The story of the prodigal son found in Luke 15:11–32 is all too familiar to these parents.

The prodigals will return…it's just a matter of time. The hard part is in the waiting, not knowing the circumstances surrounding your child. Taking our hands off of our children and waiting on the King to move in their life is oh so hard to do. We place our children on the proverbial altar letting God do what God does, only to eventually pull them back off the altar and try to control the situation on our own. The hard part is in the waiting…God will move; it says so in the story of the prodigal son in Luke 15. God does honor our grief and shows us compassion; that's the promise He makes in today's verse in Lamentations.

Jesus is calling out to our prodigals, saying, "I am calling home the sons and daughters who have forgotten Me. You will see a waterfall of love and mercy bring My children from afar. I have walled them in. They haven't roamed as far as you expected. They are never outside of the boundaries of My love, and I have never left their sides. I know how to woo the hearts I created. They cannot find what they need outside of Me. In My mercy, they will be restored with fresh passion to seek Me and to know Me.

"Dry your eyes, and with a hope-filled heart, look with eyes of faith. The lost ones are coming home. Your delight must be in finding them and loving them back into wholeness and dignity. You will remove loneliness from their hearts. You will see them restored. Even within your family, there will be healing and grace as I recapture hearts and ignite their longings for Me. Love well. Forgive completely. You will see the restoration you've prayed for. My will shall be done in their lives."

43

Can you imagine hearing Jesus speak to our prodigals in this way? Or maybe you are the prodigal. If so, let the words above penetrate your heart. Let go of all the offenses, all the hurts, all the wounds, and all the unforgiveness. It will only keep you bound up. It's time to go home. When in trouble…go home to your family. Time truly does heal all wounds. My guess is that no matter how long it's been since you first left or how long it's been since your prodigal left, the answer is the same for both cases…time heals all wounds. Trust God in the situation; let the circumstances rest in His capable hands. He has already borne the load. Jesus Himself puts it this way, "Come to Me, all you who labor and are heavy laden, and I will give you rest. Take My yoke upon you and learn from Me, for I am gentle and lowly in heart, and you will find rest for your souls. For My yoke is easy and My burden is light" (Matthew 11:28–30, NKJV).

I can promise you that there will be no rehashing the past or going back to the wound. The robe will be wrapped around the prodigal with great joy, and a feast will be prepared. Oh, what a joyous day that will be…whether you are the prodigal or the parent, healing is available for both. No matter how lost your child is, God can find them. Are you ready to go home? Or are you ready to wrap your arms around your prodigal?

Jesus, I am asking You right now to send our prodigals home. Let them see Your face and hear Your voice, and help them find their way back home to their families that love and cherish them! As we watch the road ahead, help us know You will return them safely to us. In Jesus' mighty name. Amen.

DAY 14:

"Let Him Lead You"

"Yes, this is our God, our great God forever. He will lead us onward until the end, through all time, beyond death, and into eternity!"

Psalm 48:14 (TPT)

"When your spouse dies, your world changes. You are in mourning—feeling grief and sorrow at the loss. You may feel numb, shocked, and fearful. You may feel guilty for being the one who is still alive. At some point, you may even feel angry at your spouse for leaving you."[5] These are all normal parts of the grieving process, but you can't stay there forever. This is where you have to allow Jesus to come in these areas and heal you.

This is especially difficult for any marriage, both young and old alike. But I believe the longer you are together, the more difficult this must be. I've seen it firsthand. My in-laws were married for over sixty years when my mother-in-law passed. My father-in-law was absolutely heartbroken. She was his best friend throughout all those years. They had been through good times and bad. They even went through physical separation as he was in the United States Air Force and had served overseas for some of his missions. But, in their case, absence truly did make the heart grow fonder. I have never really experienced a couple that loved each other the way they did.

But when she passed, a part of him died with her. He was just never the same after she died. He loved his children and grandchildren dearly, but he lost track of who he was as a man. I remember one day my husband asked his dad if he had made an idol of his wife. He quickly responded with an "of course not." He went to bed that night and came downstairs the next morning, and he seemed different, lighter maybe. It appeared to me that some of the heaviness was gone. When we asked him about it, he told my husband that he had thought about what he had said and prayed about it. The Lord told him he did make his family an idol, so he repented of it and asked the Lord to forgive him. He passed away not long after that. I believe he was given an opportunity to right some wrongs, and when he completed his mission, he went home to be with the Lord and his loving wife.

It was a very long year for my husband's dad, but he kept seeking the Lord through it all. He didn't

---

5   "Martik Qarah Khanian Spouse Died after 48 Years of Marriage in the U.S.," Goftar News, posted November 7, 2021, http://goftarnews.com/martik-qarah-khanian-spouse-died-after-48-years-of-marriage-in-the-u-s/5/.

really want to be here after his wife left to go home to Jesus. Through all those years together, two things were constant in their marriage…their love for each other and their love for Jesus. Both only grew stronger with time.

As I sit here and write this devotional, I look up, and I can see a wooden decoration on the opposite wall; it's a cross with three pieces of rope intertwined into one strand. It has a Bible verse on it that says, "A cord of three strands is not easily broken" (Ecclesiastes 4:12, NIV). When one of those strands breaks, part of the union is weakened. But it's important to realize the last strand isn't some ordinary piece of rope; it's the Holy Spirit. The Holy Spirit is where the true strength comes from. The Holy Spirit bound my in-laws together for sixty years. Fortunately, they were both believers. If you and your spouse are believers, you, too, are bound together with the Holy Spirit, and He gives you strength. Every loving relationship ends in pain. It's just a fact of life. Unless your story is like that of the movie *The Notebook* and you are lucky enough to die together. (This is what my husband and I are praying for.)

One day we will see our Savior face to face, and one day in eternity, we will be married to our bridegroom in heaven. It will be a different kind of marriage, for sure. But it will be the best, and it will be a marriage to last for all eternity. While we go through a lot of pain after losing a spouse, we get to look forward to the marriage supper of the Lamb. The church will be married to its bridegroom, Jesus Christ, our Savior. Can you imagine eternity in heaven with our Savior?

Jesus, I love You. Thank You for loving me even in my brokenness. You are worthy of all my praise. In Jesus' name. Amen.

DAY 15:

"I Am the Lord Who Heals You"

"He said, 'If you will listen carefully to the voice of the Lord your God and do what is right in his sight, obeying his commands and keeping all his decrees, then I will not make you suffer any of the diseases I sent on the Egyptians; for I am the Lord who heals you.'"

Exodus 15:26 (NLT)

I woke up one day and couldn't remember my husband or my own sons. This was my new reality. A career I loved and my family I cherished above everything, all gone in one day. At least that was how it felt to me at the time. You talk about a loss…this was a great loss. My life was about to change forever!

Being diagnosed with a terminal illness is not for the weak! Being told I needed to medically retire in my late forties was a crazy idea, but if I didn't do it, my life would be shortened even more. I had my first grandbaby on the way, and I wanted to meet her and put my imprint on her tiny life. So I followed my doctor's instructions and did what I needed to meet this precious grandbaby of mine and be there for my family.

Doctor appointments, chemo, medicines, and hospital stays were part of my life now. It was so much thrown at us all at once that it almost seemed overwhelming to my husband and me, but then God stepped in.

You see, when He steps into the room, everything changes! My relationship with Him grew in a way that was so *beautiful*! Jesus showed up for me. I have a very strong type A personality with a "get 'er done" attitude, so He had to slow me down so that I could pay attention to the things He was telling me. He promises in His Word He will never leave me nor forsake me…and He didn't!

I had my first round of chemo in the hospital, and then I got to meet my granddaughter for the first time. Jesus even let me be there during her birth! I remember looking into her tiny face, and I knew it was only by the grace of my Lord that I was able to hold her. Then I started praying more bodacious prayers! "Lord, if You allowed me to be with her now, I want *more* life! You can give me more. I will *not* die; I will live and declare Your works! Do it again, God!" Then my next grandbaby came…then my next. It's been ten long years of chemo and infusions, but here I am to testify to the goodness of Jesus! In all these years, I have not heard the word remission as many other vasculitis warriors have. But I am believing He is going to completely heal me of this nasty disease! He is still healing today! Receive His healing wherever you may need it…spirit, soul, or body.

Sometimes a loss is not a physical death, but it's a loss of a life we planned or the way we think our life should have turned out. This can come through a sickness, like it did for me, or through something else. Think of a homeless person; they never thought they would end up homeless. Or what about an addict? They didn't wake up one day and decide to be bound to a substance, to alcohol, to money, or to power. It just happens. It's how you respond to the unexpected that makes all the difference. We can wallow in self-pity, or we can choose to be an overcomer. Life comes at us fast! You can only do so much to prepare for the unexpected. There will come a point in your life through a loss of a loved one, a loss of the life you thought you would live through the loss of a career, or some other type of loss when you must decide to pick up your sword and fight.

You have picked up this devotional for a reason. You, too, have likely experienced a loss in your life. Healing in your life will come, but my question for you is this…are you going to fight for healing? Or are you going to wallow in self-pity?

Jesus, I am so grateful for Your healing. You are Jehovah Rapha, and You are who Your Word says You are. I will trust You always as I wait for my healing to manifest! In Yeshua's mighty name. Amen.

DAY 16:

"From Dust to Life"

"All go to one place: all are from the dust, and all return to dust."

Ecclesiastes 3:20 (NKJV)

This is a verse that settles well with my soul. I remember the story of Adam and Eve in the garden and how God made man from the dust of the earth. It says in Genesis 2:7 (NKJV), "And the LORD God formed man of the dust of the ground, and breathed into his nostrils the breath of life; and man became a living soul." But the Word also says, "But now, O Lord, You are our Father; We are the clay, and You our potter; And all we are the work of Your hand" (Isaiah 64:8,NKJV).

But then the Father reminded me of some basic science. What is needed to make clay from dust? The answer is water…in our case, the Living Water (as described in John 4:10) as Jesus described Himself. Without water the clay will eventually return to dust. So, too, we also will return to dust one day when our time on this earth is done.

"Think about how much of an end it feels like when someone dies. No matter how well we take care of ourselves and those we love, no matter how good we are, no matter how mature in the faith we become, we will not escape the reality that death is certain."[6] We all have an expiration date. I think we've all probably been to a funeral where someone declares that we are of dust and to dust we will return. I was never sure how that statement was to bring us any comfort when we experience the loss of a loved one.

> *That can certainly make us step back and wonder, What is the point of all this? In the end, we all die, decay, and decompose into dust. But for those who believe in Jesus Christ—the Living Water—as the Lord of their lives, this isn't the end but the beginning of a transformation we all long to experience. Physical death is the only way to start the process of receiving our heavenly bodies that will never wear out, decay in any way, or ever be reduced to dust.[7]*

As a believer in Jesus Christ, you will be rewarded one day with your heavenly body…no more dust, no more clay, no more decay, only life! What a glorious thought that is…can I get an *amen*?

Then I read this:

---

6 Lysa Terkeurst, "It's Not Supposed to Be This Way: Dust," https://faithgateway.com/blogs/christian-books/its-not-supposed-to-be-this-way-dust.
7 Terkeurst, "It's Not Supposed to Be This Way: Dust."

For we know that if our earthly house, this tent, is destroyed, we have a building from God, a house not made with hands, eternal in the heavens. For in this we groan, earnestly desiring to be clothed with our habitation which is from heaven, if indeed, having been clothed, we shall not be found naked. For we who are in this tent groan, being burdened, not because we want to be unclothed, but further clothed, that mortality may be swallowed up by life. Now He who has prepared us for this very thing is God, who also has given us the Spirit as a guarantee. So we are always confident, knowing that while we are at home in the body we are absent from the Lord. We are confident, yes, well pleased rather to be absent from the body and to be present with the Lord.

2 Corinthians 5:1–6, 8 (NKJV)

While you may be experiencing great pain from the loss of a loved one, this verse and many others in God's Word clearly provide the hope of healing and of restoration with those who have traveled the road ahead of us. There is hope after brokenness! Allow your heart to hope again! Are you ready to take your next step on the road toward healing?

Jesus, I need You right now in this situation. I need to feel You, Holy Spirit. I know I will return to You one day, but today please take all my brokenness and heal me. Come for Your daughter, Lord. In Jesus' mighty name. Amen.

DAY 17:

"Jesus, Only You Can Save My Life"

Are any of you sick? You should call for the elders of the church to come and pray over you, anointing you with oil in the name of the Lord. Such a prayer offered in faith will heal the sick, and the Lord will make you well. And if you have committed any sins, you will be forgiven. Confess your sins to each other and pray for each other so that you may be healed. The earnest prayer of a righteous person has great power and produces wonderful results.

James 5:14–16 (NLT)

The words every woman dreads to hear after the sonogram are, "I'm sorry—there is no heartbeat." When we find out there is no heartbeat and we have carried this baby to full term or we have to deliver our baby knowing he or she will be born silent is such a hard thing to go through. The first thing my heart says is, "Call the elders of the church. Let's anoint this situation and watch my Jesus do a miracle," but what if it is not what happens?

Everything about your pregnancy was progressing beautifully. There was nothing abnormal or unusual in any way. You go in for a normal checkup and a routine sonogram. The tech begins the procedure, as normal, trying to locate the baby's heartbeat inside your womb. But things suddenly shift, and the tech begins making a lot more movement with the sonogram wand than normal. She gets this odd look on her face and becomes very quiet. There's no small talk, no laughing…there's nothing but silence. She quickly leaves the room, and the doctor comes in and begins to take over the sonogram. The doctor, too, is moving the wand quickly as if looking for treasure. But the treasure cannot be found. There is no heartbeat, and the doctor asks the tech to leave the room and informs you the baby was unable to survive.

This beautiful, normal pregnancy quickly becomes a nightmare! The doctor begins to discuss your options to deliver a stillborn baby or to have a cesarian section to remove the baby from your womb. The mood in the doctor's office becomes so surreal and somber. At points the silence is deafening. You may have even been at this appointment without your husband because it was just a normal checkup and everything up to this point was textbook. You're sitting there having to decide how you want to handle giving birth to a baby that will never breathe the air on this side of heaven.

If you decide to deliver the baby, you still go through all the "normal" parts of birth. You still go into labor and delivery. You still experience the pain of birthing a child. But the atmosphere is totally different from delivering a healthy baby. There is no joy. There is no sound of a baby's cry piercing the air. There is only silence and the sounds of a medical procedure. Your body even responds as if it has given birth to a healthy child. Your breasts will produce milk for a time. You still have the pain of the birth to deal with, but it seems to be worse because of the pain of a broken heart that you are also experiencing. Once the delivery is over, you get to spend a short time with the baby you were expecting to raise. You only get a few moments to say your goodbyes, to dress your baby for the first and last time, and to tell them how much you loved them before the funeral home comes to prepare your baby for burial.

The scenario described above happens all too often. The women who go through this experience have a feeling of numbness, despair, depression, and a myriad of other emotions. There may even be anger at God over their loss. All of this is normal when delivering a stillborn baby. While your emotions are high, it's important to understand that healing must begin. Allow yourself to feel the pain and the sadness for a season. But remember seasons pass, and so must your grief. You cannot become consumed with grief. This is where it is vital to your health, mentally and physically, to speak with trusted advisors and/or counselors. Put yourself in the company of others who can identify with your pain. Above all, invite God into this place of woundedness and ask Him to heal you from the inside out. Do not isolate from family and friends during this time. There is hope on the other side of brokenness. Have you invited Jesus into your wound?

Jesus, heal my broken heart as I give my baby over to You. Help me try to not figure out every area of my life right now and just sit with You. I need You, and I just need You. Amen.

DAY 18:

"Don't Be Afraid"

"But when Jesus heard what had happened, he said to Jairus, 'Don't be afraid. Just have faith, and she will be healed.'"

Luke 8:50 (NLT)

Today's subject is controversial and touchy, especially in the Christian faith. But God doesn't see it that way…Christians, however, do see it that way. It's unfortunate but true. Personally, I have never had an abortion, but I have encountered many women who have had an abortion. This subject creates a clear line in the sand for most people. You are on one side of the fence or the other. Because of this, many women feel awfully alone and ashamed later in life. I don't have statistics to tell you the number of women who regret having had an abortion or numbers for those who have no regret. The truth is the numbers don't matter. This book is all about the journey to healing after a loss. An abortion is a loss no matter how you define it or the circumstances surrounding it.

Most of the women I personally know or who have come through our ministry, Angels in Waiting 91:4, fall into the camp of having regret and shame. In actuality, it's not always about the regret of the act itself as much as it is about being unable to forgive themselves for what they have done. For those of you who are in this place in life, I want you to fully understand that Jesus died on a cross for all your sins, including the abortion you may have had. Jesus forgave you the very moment you repented and asked for forgiveness. If Jesus forgave you, and He certainly did, who are you to hold onto sin that Jesus has already forgotten? You being unwilling to forgive yourself puts yourself in the position of God. I am willing to bet that you have probably never thought of it in these terms. I'm just giving you a different perspective on unforgiveness of self. You may have to forgive yourself every day of your life or maybe even moment by moment.

Let me give you another perspective to think about it. God will not ask you to do something He hasn't already done! He had to give His Son up to deathbed also. But make no mistake—I am not saying God sinned by allowing Jesus to go to the cross for you and for me. Free will is involved in this world, whether with Jesus or with you. Jesus chose to be crucified in order that we may live with Him in eternity. That was the only way we could be atoned for our sins. You, too, had free will in your decisions. Your decision did not produce the same kind of result as Jesus', but free will was at the root of both deci-

53

sions. When God speaks, everything has to line up with His Word! My point here is that God loved you enough to give His Son up for you (see John 3:16). Shouldn't you love God enough to forgive yourself?

Your baby may have never taken a breath on this earth but will experience an eternity in heaven. All aborted babies are hoping and praying for their mommies to someday come walking through the gates of heaven. Your baby is waiting for you! Let that sink in…you have to let go of unforgiveness to get into the gates of heaven, but your baby is waiting for you there.

"Listen, my radiant one—if you ever lose sight of me, just follow in my footsteps where I lead my lovers. Come with your burdens and cares. Come to the place near the sanctuary of my shepherds" (Song of Songs 1:8, TPT). Bring your burdens, bring your cares, bring everything that is hurting you to Him. He wants to free you from the bondage that you've created for yourself. In Isaiah 61 it says He came to set the captives free.

Release your grip on your own unforgiveness and realize that you are forgiven by the King of kings and Lord of lords. Unforgiveness will only hold you in a self-made prison with no possibility of parole. You made a mistake—repent and give it to God and let go of the unforgiveness you hold for yourself. Nobody is perfect, and your sin is no different than mine. The ground is level at the foot of the cross. Do you want to be free of all your sins?

King Jesus, help me to forgive myself of my shame and regret. Come, Jesus, Your daughter awaits You with open arms. I wait expectantly until I get to see You face to face and finally meet my precious baby. In Jesus' mighty name. Amen.

DAY 19:

"Man of Sorrow"

He is despised and rejected by men, A Man of sorrows and acquainted with grief. And we hid, as it were, our faces from Him; He was despised, and we did not esteem Him. Surely He has borne our griefs And carried our sorrows; Yet we esteemed Him stricken, Smitten by God, and afflicted. But He was wounded for our transgressions, He was bruised for our iniquities; The chastisement for our peace was upon Him, And by His stripes we are healed.

Isaiah 53:3–5 (NKJV)

In many families that have experienced the loss of a baby, the daddies are often an afterthought. All eyes and words of comfort are mostly directed to the mother. But the truth is all family members are affected by this kind of loss. We did not want to lose sight of the other family members. Daddies may feel neglected or even unwanted after this kind of loss. Their pain can be every bit as deep as Mommy's. Truthfully, most men feel as though they must hold everything together even when it seems like the world is falling apart.

While the pain may be slightly different, the hurt goes just as deep. Daddy lost his baby too. Let's not forget that the baby is an impression of both the mommy and the daddy. Daddy is void of the life that he helped create. So where does Daddy turn when he is hurting too? I hate stereotyping, but in general it sometimes works. For the most part, a daddy doesn't want to show any kind of weakness. A daddy feels respected and strong when others view him as the pillar of the family, an immovable force of strength. When he takes a major blow, such as losing his child, a crack in the armor may appear.

Daddy, God wants you to know He sees you! He knows your pain better than anybody. His Son died on a cross for all humanity. Even though Jesus died for righteous reasons, it didn't make the Father hurt any less watching it from heaven. The Father identifies with your pain. It is not weakness when you share with someone the pain you are feeling. Let's remember the veil in the temple was rent in two from top to bottom when His Son gave up His life. The Father felt anger, hurt, and, I think, disappointment in His children that killed His Son.

I bet these may be some of the same emotions that you felt when you lost your child. You matter too…you are important, and you are not less than Mommy. Take all your emotions and your wounded-ness to Him. Express what you feel and invite Him into the wound. Men often place a Band-Aid over a wound that is more serious in nature. Without proper attention to the wound, a more serious problem can result. Deep infection can and will occur if the wound is not properly cared for. The infection will take your life if you allow it to fester. The wound in your heart is no different. If you put on a brave face while the pain is raging inside you, left untreated, the enemy will take your life…spiritually and physically.

I also encourage you to speak with someone else who has experienced the same thing you are going through now. It doesn't have to be a professional therapist. But it does need to be someone you trust, someone who will manage your heart with care. God uses people to speak into our lives. As a man, you should know it's not weakness to share how you feel or to shed a tear or two. In fact, I would say that makes you even stronger.

I will caution you, however, not to stay caught up in your feelings. My daddy used to tell me, "It's okay to get down—just don't stay down. Pick yourself up, dust yourself off, and put one foot in front of the other. Keep moving forward no matter what. There will be better days; your best is yet to come." God will move you forward if you put your trust in Him. He has a plan for your life, and it doesn't include weakness. You are a warrior man of God. Are you ready to armor up?

Father God, I pray right now for any daddy who is hurting and trying to find his way through this trial. Lord, wrap Your arms around him and give him the strength he needs to endure this race. In Jesus' name. Amen.

DAY 20:

"Give Me Peace for the Moment"

"You number my wanderings; Put my tears into Your bottle; Are they not in Your book?"

Psalm 56:8 (NKJV)

One of our founding members is the designer of the girl angel gown. She has chosen to design the girl gowns because she has two baby girls in heaven. She does this in remembrance of her two daughters.

She was planning on the arrival of her first baby in 1969 when she started experiencing back pain and went to the doctor. She was told then it was probably just pressure from the baby and to put a board under her mattress. She was told these were normal pains, but it turned out that these pains were anything but normal…she was having pain due to premature labor. She was seven and a half months pregnant at the time when she had a stillborn baby girl. She later had a rainbow baby…a baby girl, her first healthy baby. Her outlook turned from despair to motherhood with the joy of her little girl in her life.

But this was not the end of her story. About ten years later, she was ready to give birth to her third child. Everything was progressing normally with a strong heartbeat all the way through the pregnancy. She went to the ER due to a gallbladder attack, and they performed an ultrasound. The size of the baby was growing rapidly, and there were some concerns, so the doctors were cautious. She was told by the doctor after the results of the ultrasound had come back that her baby was a water-head baby, also known as hydrocephalus. The doctors told her at that time the baby would die at birth or shortly thereafter. The baby weighed twelve pounds and thirteen ounces, and they wrapped her in a hospital sheet to protect Mommy from seeing her baby's large head. The nurses covered the head and only allowed her to see the face. They told her she looked like a Gerber baby. This was such an act of kindness on their part. Fortunately, she was able to deliver another healthy baby girl shortly after the second stillbirth, her fourth child.

The mother of these two babies was not a Christian when she gave birth to these children. She struggled with the death of these two babies and was looking for someone to blame. She thought she was being punished because of her mother having her illegitimately and didn't want her because of it. She was angry, sad, and hurt, blaming her family for years for the pain she was experiencing. She was raised by a loving and protective grandmother. She grew up in church but would later walk away from her faith.

Fortunately, God brought two beautiful rainbow babies who caused the pain of the past to become somewhat more manageable. She still did not understand the loss of her first two daughters, and the grief never really subsided. She lived with the pain for quite some time, and then she met Jesus for the first time in her life. The joy her daughters brought into her life still didn't bring fulfillment because it was Jesus she was looking for. Her grief was a form of validation; it said the wound mattered. Her children's lives mattered to her.

But God will heal these wounds if we only bring them to Him. God will bring goodness and beauty from all our trials and tears. His Word says so. It tells us He will give us beauty for ashes, oil of joy for mourning, the garment of praise for the spirit of heaviness, that they might be called oaks of righteousness, the planting of Adonai that He may be glorified (Isaiah 61:3). As it says in today's verse in Psalm 56:8, He collects our tears, and He uses them to produce something beautiful.

Sometimes we are only able to see the piece of the picture that is closest to us. We fail to see the whole masterpiece. But if you look to Jesus instead of the problem, you will see the complete picture. You will be able to see the whole picture. I think of Peter when Jesus invited him to walk upon the troubled waters. If you look at the water, it will hide the picture. But if you look at Jesus, the little piece that looks so ominous to you must shrink back into place allowing you to see the peace and the calm instead of the troubled waters all around you. Are you ready to walk on troubled waters with Him?

Jesus, I pray for everyone reading this that You will heal them from the things they have been said or done to them that no one has ever apologized for. Help them to forgive. Heal the wounds of our past and make a beautiful garden out of their tears. Do what only You can do, Lord. In Jesus' name. Amen.

DAY 21:

"Jesus Hears Us"

Return and tell Hezekiah the leader of My people, "Thus says the Lord, the God of David your father: 'I have heard your prayer, I have seen your tears; surely I will heal you. On the third day you shall go up to the house of the Lord. And I will add to your days fifteen years. I will deliver you and this city from the hand of the king of Assyria; and I will defend this city for My own sake, and for the sake of My servant David.'"

2 Kings 20:5–6 (NKJV)

Did you know Jesus hears you when you pray to Him? Let's just think for a minute—the God of this universe turns His ears to hear your prayers. When I decided to follow Jesus, I thought all my troubles and worries would fade away and that Jesus would hear my prayers and make it all right, but boy, was I wrong. Things seemed to get harder, and I had to pray and fast more often. God was not a genie in a magic bottle I could rub and everything would be okay. I had to learn to travail in prayer and keep my face on the ground near His feet. I had to cry out to Him and believe He is who He says He is. Either the Bible is the truth, or it is a lie. I found out during my walk with Him that He is who the Word says He is and He can and will do what His Word says He will do. I find great strength in knowing Him for His Word!

Following Jesus will cost you everything! And I mean everything…friends, family, and church members. In Luke 14:25–33 Jesus is telling the great multitudes who were following Him to be sure to count the cost. So let's take a quick look at the bookends of this passage—verses 26 and 33. Verse 26 (NKJV) says, "If anyone comes to Me and does not hate his father and mother, wife and children, brothers and sisters, yes, and his own life also, he cannot be My disciple." And He states a similar sentiment in verse 33 (NKJV), "So likewise, whoever of you does not forsake all that he has cannot be My disciple." Jesus is making it clear that the cost of being a disciple of Christ is very costly. You give up all that you think you are and be willing to give up all you have for Him.

I look at it like a grape that has to be crushed to make wine. Your anointing is the crushing, and not everyone will understand why you are willing to go through this painful and agonizing process. But let me tell you—once you meet Him and hear His voice, all the troubles of the world are so worth this process. Though it can be very painful and lonely, my reward will be Him one day in heaven, where all this world is left behind. In the warfare you will have to wage—do not make light of your enemy's strength, for the odds are all against you, and you had better see to it that, despite every disadvantage, you still have the wherewithal to hold out and win the day. Life is crushing at times. The devil has a way of using our pain and heartache against us. Satan is an accuser of the brethren. So be sure to keep the words that come out of your mouth positive. The devil likes nothing more than to use our own words against us. If you can't say anything positive, don't say anything at all.

Jesus will hear your cries for help! He will step into your circumstances when the time is right and not a minute before or a minute too late. First John 5:14–15 (NKJV) says, "Now this is the confidence that we have in Him, that if we ask anything according to His will, He hears us. And if we know that He hears us, whatever we ask, we know that we have the petitions that we have asked of Him." That is a promise straight from Jesus! We do have the responsibility to ask with a right heart; He will not honor prayers that are condemning or hateful. Be sure to keep your heart in alignment with His Word. Did you catch what John said in 1 John 5:14? You must ask according to His will, not yours. He expects us to have a clean heart, not a vengeful or condemning heart. But if you truly love the Lord with all your heart, all your soul, and all your strength, then your heart will be good and full of light. Loving God produces light in every area of our life. So cry out to Him; He hears you. If you were sitting down with Jesus today, what would you say to Him?

Jesus, I come to You today and ask You to make my heart pure toward anything I might be trying to carry. Help me and save me from the thoughts and words that have been spoken over me. I confess I need You. In Jesus' name. Amen.

DAY 22:

"I Will Wait for You"

He gives power to the weak, And to those who have no might He increases strength. Even the youths shall faint and be weary, And the young men shall utterly fall, But those who wait on the Lord Shall renew their strength; They shall mount up with wings like eagles, They shall run and not be weary, They shall walk and not faint.

Isaiah 40:29–31 (NKJV)

How's your hope level, friends? In this time when everything is chaotic, when there's more month than money, and there just doesn't seem to be any rest. It's easy to lose hope nowadays. But take heart, my friends. Jesus is home to the hopeless. The Lord says it like this in the book of Isaiah, "He gives power to the weak, and to those who have no might He increases strength…they shall run and not grow weary, they will walk and not be faint" (Isaiah 40:29, 31, NKJV). We become hopeful when we look at what God can do, not at what man has done. Hope emerges within us when we focus on the capabilities of God rather than the inability of man. Hope springs up when we praise God for His perfection—acknowledging and trusting in all that He is.

If you are exhausted and weary at the end of the day, shut yourself in for a while with God. Praise Him with every ounce of your being and with all the energy that remains in you. You will find yourself refreshed, not only mentally and emotionally, but physically. There is a special strength imparted to those who praise the Lord. This kind of strength gives you the power to outlast tough times. It gives you the power to intercede until [the] breakthrough [comes].[8]

He sees you, He hears you, and He is waiting for you.

Do you ever wonder if God hears your prayers? This verse is a reminder of God's hands on our lives even when we think He is quiet. "Therefore, the Lord will wait, that He may be gracious to you; And therefore He will be exalted, that He may have mercy on you. For the Lord is a God of justice; Blessed are all those who wait for Him" (Isaiah 30:18, NKJV).

We live in a world where we don't want to wait for much of anything. But how many of us had a

---

8 Michael Youssef, "The Hope That Energizes," posted January 17, 2022, https://ca.ltw.org/read/my-devotional/2022/01/the-hope-that-energizes.

grandmother who told us, "Good things come to those who wait"? We live in a microwave society, but we serve a crock-pot God. The internet has only exacerbated the problem. We want what we want, and we want it now. We don't want to have to wait for anything. But Jesus is in the waiting. When we pray to God and He doesn't answer us right away, we get impatient and wonder what He is doing. When all along He is doing something. He is just working on you in the waiting. I have often heard it said that God does His greatest work while we are in the waiting.

Submit yourself to God while you are waiting…this is the most precious time for us. James 4:7 (NIV) says, "Submit yourselves, then, to God. Resist the devil and he will flee from you." Submit and resist, and you will see His hand over and over again in your life if you allow Him to be God. We have a part to play. Our part is to submit and resist, and God will do the rest.

This is a beautiful reminder of our sweet Jesus: "Wait on the Lord; Be of good courage, And He shall strengthen your heart; Wait, I say, on the Lord!" (Psalm 27:14, NKJV). He is working all things together for your good (see Romans 8:28). Frankly, we've made a mess of our lives, and it's going to take some time to unravel it all and for Him to get us where He needs us to be. We can wallow in self-pity when things don't go the way we think they should. Think about how long you've stayed in a funk over losing your child, your husband or wife, or your job. Whatever the case may be, we can stay in the ditch far too long. All the while God is offering us a hand to lift us out of the muck and the mire. Sometimes the first step is letting go and giving it all to God. Give Him your pain and your impatience. Invite Him into the situation.

Imagine one day your waiting will be over here, and you will walk into heaven to gaze upon the beauty of your Savior, and then He will introduce you to the child you've wondered about every day since they passed away. Your time is coming; your waiting will be over…for some situations, it could be here on earth that your waiting will end, or it could be when you arrive in heaven. The story will change. You will see your child again. You will get a new job. Your prodigal will come home. Whatever you're going through now will end…God has a way of working all things out. You have to trust in Him and be patient in the waiting. Look for Him while you're waiting, and wait expectantly! God loves it when we have expectations of Him. Are you willing to wait for God's way and get the blessings He has planned for you? Or do you want to do it your way and only get a partial reward?

Jesus, help me wait on You. In this season of life, I feel so lost. I need a Savior. I need Your help. In Jesus' name. Amen.

DAY 23:

"Just One Touch"

Wherever he went, in the countryside, villages, or towns, they placed the sick on mats in the streets or in public places and begged him, saying, "Just let us touch the tassel of your prayer shawl!" And all who touched him were instantly healed!

Mark 6:56 (TPT)

Many women suffer post-partum depression, including myself. It can start as the baby blues and turn into full-blown depression if left untreated. There is really no rhyme nor reason to who gets post-partum depression and who doesn't get it. It runs the spectrum of just a little sadness from a hormonal imbalance to extreme depression where a mother can't even hold her child or even worse.

Early recognition is very important, and you should seek medical help as soon as possible if things start to worsen. Your doctor will be able to lead you to the right treatment or send you for a consult with a psychologist if needed. Approximately one in ten women will experience post-partum depression after giving birth. If this is you, you are not alone.

Jesus is the healer of all things; there is nothing He can't do. It's important that we take all our worries and concerns to Him. Nothing is too insignificant to Him. If it's bothering you, it also bothers Him. There is nothing beyond His vision; He sees all things and knows all things. You may be able to put on a brave face for all the world to see, but God sees the true you. He may instantly remove your post-partum depression, or He may direct your path to someone He wants to use to help you. But the first step to finding healing is to admit there is a problem and release it to Him.

In essence this a loss of self. You may feel like you have lost your identity, but our true identity is in Christ. To find healing, you must find yourself in Him. You must come to the end of you to find yourself in Him. You may feel like you are rejecting your child; you may feel like you're a bad mother. But these are all lies from the enemy. You may need to give yourself grace in the moment. You cannot beat yourself up because you're not the perfect wife or the perfect mother. Let me help you out…there is no such thing as the perfect wife or perfect mother. The only thing perfect is Christ's love for you. You are accepted and approved by Him. Let go of the idea of perfection and be who God created you to be.

You are a gift to your child; you are not a mistake. The enemy swoops right in at every opportune moment to destroy what God calls "good." In 2 Corinthians 10:3–6 (NKJV) it says:

For though we walk in the flesh, we do not war according to the flesh. For the weapons of our warfare are not carnal but mighty in God for pulling down strongholds, casting down arguments and every high thing that exalts itself against the knowledge of God, bringing every thought into captivity to the obedience of Christ, and being ready to punish all dis- obedience when your obedience is fulfilled.

We must war in the spirit world against everything that comes against the goodness of God. This begins by taking captive every thought that is not of God.

The enemy seeks to infiltrate our thought life and plant seeds that will produce death and destruction. It's our responsibility as a believer to counter every vicious attack of the enemy by decreeing and declaring His Word over our particular situation. Find His promises in the Bible and speak them out…often! Our words are important. Do not speak negative words into the atmosphere. Speak only truth and life! When the enemy says you are rejected, you tell him that you are accepted and approved. You have been purchased at a very high price; you were ransomed by the blood of Jesus. The wounds in our lives will try to create a stronghold—invite Him into the wound, and He will heal it. It just takes one touch. What is the wound you are not allowing Jesus to touch?

Jesus, help me trust You and hand over every thought the enemy throws at me. You are my healer! I put all my trust in You. In Jesus' name. Amen.

DAY 24:

"Serve Him"

When Jesus went into Peter's house [in Capernaum], He saw Peter's mother-in-law lying sick in bed with a fever. He touched her hand and the fever left her; and she got up and served Him. When evening came, they brought to Him many who were under the power of demons; and He cast out the evil spirits with a word, and restored to health all who were sick [exhibiting His authority as Messiah], so that He fulfilled what was spoken by the prophet Isaiah: "He Himself took our infirmities [upon Himself] and carried away our diseases."

Matthew 8:14–17 (AMP)

Today we are going discuss a different topic…the loss of hope from the inability to have a child, an empty womb. This is a loss no matter how you define the word. It is loss of hopes and dreams; it's a loss of a biological family. Most couples enter into marriage with the hopes of having children of their own, with a few exceptions to that rule. The number of couples who want a family far outweighs those who don't, even though the trend is heading in the other direction at this time. But for those who want a baby but are unable to conceive, for whatever reason, this is devastating news.

We have come across countless couples, some in our own family, that have been unable to conceive. These couples desire to have a baby more than anything in the world. They spend thousands of dollars on the latest and greatest medical advances in hopes of conceiving, but it just never happens. These couples are often left not only without a child but sometimes are left bankrupt…financially and spiritually. Because of the spiritual bankruptcy, the potential mother bears the biggest burden in this scenario, and she can feel angry, defeated, and rejected. This doesn't have to be the case, however. Instead of turning away from God during this time, it's vitally important that you turn toward God. He is our comforter, our strength, and our guide. He can provide divine strategy to conceive, or He can lead you in another direction, aligning other avenues for you to be a parent. Remember He works all things together for our good if we love Him (see Romans 8:28).

When you first read this section of Scripture in Matthew 8, you likely wouldn't think this would be applicable to an empty womb. But I would argue to the contrary. You see, Jesus healed Peter's mother-in-law from some infirmities. It doesn't say she was dying of some terminal illness or plague-like illness, such as leprosy. All we know is that Peter must have cared deeply for his mother-in-law for her to be living in his household, and he was anxious to have her healed. Perhaps she was a better cook than his wife…just kidding. No, the miracle here was not the extraordinary miracle of resurrection or healing the blind eye or the deaf ear. But one simple touch from Jesus' hand brought this woman from the bed to serve Him and all His disciples. She showed a fitting response by immediately arising from her bed to serve. Serving Jesus is evidence of being restored to spiritual health.

Jesus can and has healed the empty womb. But you must put your trust in Him with your whole being. He is waiting for a fitting response from you. Before a vintage wine comes to the table there must be a crushing of the fruit. Going through the broken hopes and dreams of not being able to conceive is crushing to many people. But Jesus is in the miracle business and makes wine from water. Isn't that the One you want working on your behalf? So the next time you receive that devastating news that you are unable to get pregnant, instead of trying the next great medical advancement or some old wives tale remedy, put your faith in Jesus Christ. He is the anchor of your soul. He will guide you in the way you are to go, and once you are all in with your faith, He will make a way where there seems to be no way. Jesus is the door to all of your hopes and dreams. His plans often look very different than our plans, but His plans bring life and life more abundant. Jesus is not an "assembly line" kind of God cranking out miracle after miracle that all are the same. Jesus treats us individually at the point of our need. He responds to our needs. Think about the leper that Jesus healed by the touch of His hand. That leper hadn't been touched by anybody in any way for a very long time. The touch of Christ not only healed the leper's body but also healed his soul. There are plenty of women in Scripture who had a barren womb. Look first to Abraham's wife, Sarah—in Genesis 17, she received the promise of being the mother of many nations, but she had to learn to trust in God's plan even after she tried to conceive her own way. Then look at Elizabeth, the mother of John the Baptist. She was an old woman when her husband, Zechariah, received word that they would have a son who would be the forerunner of the Messiah. John would herald the news of the arrival of Jesus as Messiah. Or how about Rachel? In Genesis 30:1, Rachel was desperate for a child. God answered her prayer by giving her Joseph and Benjamin, who became two of the twelve tribes of Israel. But she died giving birth to Benjamin (see Genesis 35:18). There is power in the waiting, and there is hope. Wait patiently upon the Lord and wait well. These three women from the Bible are not the only stories of the barren womb. There are others. Search the Scriptures for the case that looks most like yours and then claim the promises.

No matter the case with you, your situation or circumstance is not too small for Him. He cares about what you care about. He sees your heart and desire to be good; He sees your struggles, and He is always there to listen and help when you pray to Him with a sincere and humble heart. I love how the prophet Jeremiah puts it in Jeremiah 31:3 (NKJV), "Yes, I have loved you with an everlasting love; Therefore, with lovingkindness I have drawn you." God will do whatever it takes to draw you to Him. Submit to

Him and obey what He tells you to do, and it will go well with you. Trust Him with your dreams and allow Him to do a mighty work in your life. Are you ready to arise from your bed and serve Him?

Jesus, I pray for every barren womb right now. Lord, give them peace in this situation and lead them into Your arms and Your healing in every area of their lives. Amen.

DAY 25:

"Be Courageous"

"Be strong and of good courage, do not fear nor be afraid of them; for the Lord your God, He is the One who goes with you. He will not leave you nor forsake you."

Deuteronomy 31:6 (NKJV)

As the storms of life rage, we have this promise from God, in His Word, that "He will never leave [us] or forsake [us]" (Deuteronomy 31:6, NKJV). That is a great assurance to my heart that no matter what I walk through, I know He is with me. The storms will rage, and the waters will toss us to and fro, but Jesus…! (Ephesians 4:14) You and I must stay strong in the Lord and seek His face for answers, not the world. This world has nothing to offer you and me, my friends. Learning to trust in the season you are in can be very difficult. You must be close enough to the Savior to hear His voice and obey. He is worthy of all our trust!

But He has made us such a *beautiful* promise in Deuteronomy 31:6. Are you standing on "His" promises? I am breathing in "His" promises, and I am believing "He" is who "He" says "He" is! "He" is *the Great I Am*! That gives me so much *faith* and *hope* for my future! Stay in the Word of God and listen to "His" small voice. Let "Him" lead you and surrender all your fears to "Him"…"He" already took all our sins on that ole rugged cross for you and me!

There are times, like during the loss of a loved one, when we can't feel Him or His Word. This usually means there is something blocking the way of Him. It could be the desires of the flesh or the pursuit of other things to try to comfort ourselves. It is easy for the world to pull us off the path that leads to Him. He never moves; He never changes. He is the same yesterday, today, and forever. We are the ones that move away from Him.

But God is always faithful. I was reminded of His presence as the wind blew so lightly upon my face today. This was a gentle reminder that Jesus is in everything! But sometimes we must take time to slow down and see Him even in the smallest of things. "The Lord will watch over your coming and going both now and forevermore!" (Psalm 121:8, NIV). He is waiting for you…won't you notice Him? Take time to appreciate all the beauty He placed in your life. Go outside and hear the birds chirping. Stand in a gentle shower feeling the raindrops on your face. He is *everywhere* if we just open our eyes and look for Him.

We don't have to have all the answers. He wants you to come to Him when you are hurting, when you are confused, and even when you are mad at Him. He just wants you to come to Him. He wants to spend time with you. He wants to love on you and give you peace! He is the source of *all* things. Recognize Him for who He is…He is the *Great I Am*.

He is the only One who has the answers. Our precious Jesus is willing and able to do much more than we could ever imagine (Ephesians 3:20). Do you trust Him when the storms are raging? Do you run to Him or the world?

> *Lord, I know there will always be storms around me, but I know when I have You, I am safe. Jesus, please keep me in Your hands, where I know that as the storms of life come, my safe place is with You. I love You, Lord. In Jesus' mighty name. Amen.*

DAY 26:

"I Have Seen Him"

"I have seen his ways, and will heal him; I will also lead him, And restore comforts to him And to his mourners. 'I create the fruit of the lips: Peace, peace to him who is far off and to him who is near,' Says the Lord, 'And I will heal him.'"

Isaiah 57:18–19 (NKJV)

First and foremost, God did not cause your baby to die. It was not His will to take your baby to heaven. Many times in life, when we find ourselves in situations like these, we hear many words either spoken over us or even spoken by us. The Bible makes it clear life and death are in the power of the tongue (Proverbs 18:21). It is vitally important how we speak if we want to live a blessed life. Let's be clear, though: a blessed life is not necessarily a trouble-free life.

Let's take a closer look at some words we may have heard after the loss of a child. "Try these terms" and "weren't very far along in your pregnancy." Whether you are deep into your pregnancy or not, you still lost your baby. They were important to you, and they mattered. Or this one…"Don't worry—you should still be able to have another baby." First, how can anyone be sure of that, and second, what about this baby? Then this is a classic example too…"God must have needed another little angel in heaven." This makes it sound like my little baby is floating around heaven with a pair of wings and is playing a harp on a cloud. They are angelic beings clearly defined separately from human beings. My baby is not an angel.

Hopefully, you can see how hurtful these words can be. We must learn to speak words that produce fruit, words that speak life and love, words that comfort and heal. "Think before you speak" is good advice in these situations. In the Bible, there are decrees, declarations, and curses. There can be curses of death, curses on our finances, curses on our relationships, and even curses on our health. Curses can be spoken, unspoken, or transferred to us through a variety of means or even by our own behavior, thoughts, and attitudes.

The enemy will use whatever means he can to take our life. He hates you because God created you to be on a higher level than him. He only wanted to be higher and more powerful than God, and when God created mankind to be higher than angels…in short, Lucifer got very full of himself, and that resulted in his eviction from heaven. He has been mad about it ever since and has sought to destroy us because we came from God, and we are created in His image. The enemy hates that fact. In John 10:10, it says that he came to steal, kill, and destroy. He will use whatever means at his disposal, and he will use whoever will take the bait to speak death and destruction over us. In short, that is the enemy's goal.

But God has given us some tools to defeat the enemy and to cancel the words spoken over us. All throughout the Bible are promises that we should be declaring and decreeing over our lives. Here is a great example of declaring God's Word over our lives: "I now claim every spiritual blessing that my Heavenly Father has given to me in Christ Jesus (Ephesians 1:3). I claim those blessings right here in the very place of all cursing, by the authority and power of the Lord Jesus Christ and in His name."[9]

Speak the Word of God over your life. Find meaningful scriptures that are especially important to you and speak them out over your life. There is healing, life, and peace available to you. But you must speak it out. His Word will do the work! What has been spoken over you that needs to be canceled?

Father God, help me to speak words that edify myself and others around me. I confess I can't do this without You! I need Your guidance in all things, especially forgiving those who have broken my heart with their hurtful words. Come, Lord Jesus, and heal areas in my heart that others can't see that are still bleeding. In Jesus' mighty name. Amen.

---

9 "Prayer for Breaking Curses," Wild at Heart, https://wildatheart.org/prayer/prayer-breaking-curses#:~:text=I%20now%20claim%20every%20spiritual,Christ%2C%20and%20in%20his%20name.

DAY 27:

"The Table"

The Lord is my shepherd; I shall not want. He makes me to lie down in green pastures; He leads me beside the still waters. He restores my soul; He leads me in the paths of righteousness For His name's sake. Yea, though I walk through the valley of the shadow of death, I will fear no evil; For You are with me; Your rod and Your staff, they comfort me. You prepare a table before me in the presence of my enemies; You anoint my head with oil; My cup runs over. Surely goodness and mercy shall follow me All the days of my life; And I will dwell in the house of the Lord Forever.

Psalm 23:1–6 (NKJV)

I am reminded that a table has a great value to a family. It holds around it everyone we hold dear to our hearts. What must the day we celebrate the great banquet with Jesus be like? I can only imagine what a day that will be like! I can *only* imagine seeing Jesus face to face! Oh, what a *glorious* day that shall be! To sit, or should I say fall to my knees, in the presence of our *King* Jesus! I am reminded in the Bible in Psalm 23:5 (NKJV), which says, "You prepare a table before me in the presence of my enemies; You anoint my head with oil; My cup runs over." Let's read that again: He prepares a table before me in the presence of *my* enemies! Dear friends, let that sink in for a minute. That table of His…He puts us around it with Him! God put His children around His very own table just like we do with the ones we love and hold so dearly to our hearts! Are you getting it? He truly *loves* us that much! The Savior of the world is inviting us to sit at His table! That is so very humbling to me. How about you? My prayer for you today is that you seek His face in such a way that you don't want anything from *Him* but all of *Him*. Sit or lie at the feet of Jesus and just look at His nail-scarred feet and remember what He gave for *you*! He gave all!

He placed me in a seat at the table where I don't belong. There's nothing I can do to earn my place at His great banquet table. In my deepest pain, He sweeps me away in His love. I don't see my brokenness anymore when I'm seated at His table. You place me in a place of honor even when I don't deserve a seat. You have prepared a place for me. My mind cannot comprehend it; it's too wonderful for me to fathom.

We always tend to think of Psalm 23 as a song of sadness because it is often associated with funerals. But there is such hope and life in these scriptures. I hope you can see that from just the description of God Himself preparing a place for you at the table. But there is so much more to this Psalm. There is no lack, no need when we are in Him. He has given us everything…we shall not want. He fulfills all our desires. Secondly, He leads us into places of peace and tranquility. We can rest in Him when the world comes crashing in all around us. Even when we do go through difficult times, we can trust that He is always with and that His perfect love drives out all fear. Even His correction and discipline are a comfort to us. He gives us a fresh anointing, pouring fresh oil into our lives to the point of overflow, with goodness and mercy as my backup, following me all the days of my life. Does it get any better than that?

Grief is the price we pay for love…yes. Love always ends. Whether we spend our life loving a spouse or a child leaving us before their time or the parent leaving the child. Nothing really prepares you for the ending of love. But Psalm 23 makes it clear that God is always looking out for us and will lead us through the rough places. He is beckoning you now to "come sit at the table with Me; I've prepared a place just for you." Is your grief stopping you from sitting at the table with Him?

Father, I am eternally grateful You have chosen me. Even when I don't feel worthy of Your love, You come and prepare the table for me. I love You, Jesus. Amen.

DAY 28:

"If I Could Just Touch His Robe"

Just then a woman who had suffered for twelve years with constant bleeding came up behind him. She touched the fringe of his robe, for she thought, "If I can just touch his robe, I will be healed." Jesus turned around, and when he saw her he said, "Daughter, be encouraged! Your faith has made you well." And the woman was healed at that moment.

Matthew 9:20–22 (NLT)

In your pain, have you cried out to God for your healing? What would you be willing to do if the Healer was in the room with you? These are just two questions that come to mind when reading this familiar passage of Scripture. How did you react after receiving the news that you would not be taking home the baby but having to make funeral arrangements instead? Your entire spirit, soul, and body, your heart, mind, and will are in unbearable pain during this time. Healing from this wound might seem impossible to you, especially early after your loss. Some, even after a long period of time, still can't find healing.

Whether your loss is still fresh in your heart or occurred many years ago, the pain is just as real if you haven't invited God into the wound. The woman with the issue of blood had suffered for twelve long years. She spent nearly every penny she had to get help. She went to doctors and religious men seeking healing, all the while bearing the stigma of an outcast. She tried desperately to hide her problem. But I am sure there were moments when someone noticed the issue. Instead of getting sympathy, they yelled at her and sent her into the wilderness on her own. No one to go with her, no one to share her pain, no one to sympathize with her. She was treated as a leper would have been treated…ostracized from society. She likely hadn't felt the touch of anyone in over twelve years. Can you imagine how alone you would feel? She would have given anything to be healed. But then she heard about Jesus. She heard of His miracles, and she probably heard of His great love. She made up her mind to go find Him. She was willing to do anything. She lost her family, she lost her friends, and she lost hope until she saw Him! She took a leap of faith to press through the crowds surrounding Jesus to simply touch the hem of His garment.

Are you desperate enough for healing that you are willing to do anything to find hope again, to experience peace again, to simply live life again without the pain and the hurt? You simply must seek Him in the midst of your pain. There's only one place where you can find healing. There's only one person who can bring true peace and comfort to you. Jesus is the only One who can truly identify with your pain because He bore that pain on the cross. Jesus felt your pain as He hung by nails for you. He will bring healing, but we have to invite Him into the pain. Our Savior is a gentleman and will not come where He is not wanted.

Let's return to our story found in Matthew 9. Let's take a closer look at the character of Jesus. These couple of verses above are only part of the story. You see, Jesus was on His way to heal a little girl of one of the rulers. The ruler also knew that one touch by Jesus would heal his daughter. The crowds had heard about Jesus and were clogging the streets making it difficult for Him to get to where He needed to go…the ruler's home. It was during this time that Jesus stopped in the middle of the road because He felt the power go out of Him. Jesus simply wanted to know who touched Him so He could let them know beyond a shadow of a doubt that they were healed, and that is exactly what He did.

But then Jesus went to complete His mission…healing the ruler's daughter. The servants in the ruler's house came to Him and told Him to leave Jesus alone; his daughter was already dead. This did not deter Jesus in the least, however. He moved forward knowing that He would raise her back to life.

Jesus may not have raised your child from the dead, but He can bring *you* back to life. Will you invite Him into the pain, into your wound?

Jesus, as You pass by me many times in the day, I pray I can always touch the hem of Your garment because that is where my healing begins and ends…with You. I may not truly understand all this pain I am going through, but I can trust the One who is with me at all times. Thank You, Lord, for choosing me before I was formed in my mother's womb. I praise You, Lord. In Jesus' name. Amen.

DAY 29:

"Rest in Me"

"And everything I've taught you is so that the peace which is in me will be in you and will give you great confidence as you rest in me. For in this unbelieving world you will experience trouble and sorrows, but you must be courageous, for I have conquered the world!"

John 16:33(TPT)

During a time of loss, such as losing a baby, whether as a miscarriage, a stillbirth, or soon after birth, everything seems to be a whirlwind or total chaos. Finding peace in the middle of chaos is seemingly impossible. But as with everything in our human, finite minds, peace is available; we just have to have eyes to see. Every hurricane has an eye where there is peace and calm. The winds will be blowing frantically on the outer portions of the hurricane, but inside the eye there is nothing but utter calmness. Once you leave the eye of the storm, you can be easily swept away by the ferocious winds. It's the same with the spiritual storms in our lives; as long as we stay close to God, His shalom (peace) will envelop us. We must draw near to His heart to stay protected from all the chaos all around us.

No matter how vicious your battle, draw near to God. He will bring you peace no matter what it may look like on the outside. Stay anchored in Jesus. Do not allow the demands of your situation to pull you away. Pastors and ministry leaders often take a sabbatical to draw near to God in order to be more effective for the kingdom. You may need your own sabbatical of sorts in order to find the heart or spirit of God.

God can't reveal anything to us if we don't have His Spirit. How many times do we say, "If only God would tell me what to do"? Well, I have good news for you, friends…Jesus is talking to you. The problem is we are not listening; we are too busy or distracted. Other things are taking His place in our lives. Take some time today to stop and be still with Him and allow Him to speak to you. Just sit in His presence and breath Him in. I love Psalm 46:10 (NKJV): "Be still, and know that I am God; I will be exalted among the nations, I will be exalted in the earth!" How beautiful is that verse! Just be still…with Him.

Then as you sit with Him, you will begin to look more like Him and want more and more of Him. Then you can ask yourself, *Does my life look like Jesus?* Being in His presence and listening to His voice is the only way. I was reading Ephesians, and I happened to notice a pattern in Ephesians 1 that

I hadn't paid much attention to before. In the first fourteen verses of chapter 1, Paul uses the phrase in Christ/in Him/in Himself eight times. Why would Paul use this phrase(s) so many times? I believe he states the purpose right near the beginning in verse 4 (NKJV), where he says, "He chose us in Him before the foundation of the world." He predestined us to adoption into the family of God. Before we were ever born, we were in Him. Everything we need is found in Him. He is our source of peace…the prophet Isaiah refers to Jesus as the "Prince of Peace" in Isaiah 9:6. Again in 2 Thessalonians 3:16 (NKJV), "Now may the Lord of peace Himself give you peace always in every way. The Lord be with you all."

Resting in God is a place of total peace! You will need to protect this peace, however. The enemy does not want you to have peace because he knows when you are at peace you are near the Almighty. Near the Almighty is the last place the enemy wants you. When you are in a place of chaos and worry and depression or fear, then he can separate you from God. Have you ever watched a tribe of lions hunting? The lionesses team up to separate their prey from the herd they are traveling in. Once they separate the prey from the rest of the herd, they can then take advantage of the numbers, and the lionesses can use their superior strength to get the kill. The devil is not a creative being. The best he can do is attempt to copy nature or what God does. The same is true here when he attempts to steal your peace, your joy, and sap you of all strength. The devil's goal is to separate you from God where you are much more vulnerable to his attacks. The way you prevent this is to stay in peace by staying in Him. Do you need supernatural peace in your life today?

Lord, I need Your peace in my life. I am asking You to help me find the rest my soul needs in You. Come, Lord Jesus, and abide in me. In Jesus' name. Amen.

DAY 30:

"El Shaddai"

When you abide under the shadow of Shaddai, you are hidden in the strength of God Most High. He's the hope that holds me and the stronghold to shelter me, the only God for me, and my great confidence. He will rescue you from every hidden trap of the enemy, and he will protect you from false accusation and any deadly curse. His massive arms are wrapped around you, protecting you. You can run under his covering of majesty and hide. His arms of faithfulness are a shield keeping you from harm. You will never worry about an attack of demonic forces at night nor have to fear a spirit of darkness coming against you. Don't fear a thing! Whether by night or by day, demonic danger will not trouble you, nor will the powers of evil be launched against you. Even in a time of disaster, with thousands and thousands being killed, you will remain unscathed and unharmed. You will be a spectator as the wicked perish in judgment, for they will be paid back for what they have done! When we live our lives within the shadow of God Most High, our secret hiding place, we will always be shielded from harm. How then could evil prevail against us or disease infect us? God sends angels with special orders to protect you wherever you go, defending you from all harm. If you walk into a trap, they'll be there for you and keep you from stumbling. You'll even walk unharmed among the fiercest powers of darkness, trampling every one of them beneath your feet! For here is what the Lord has spoken to me: "Because you loved me, delighted in me, and have been loyal to my name, I will greatly protect you. I will answer your cry for help every time you pray, and you will feel my presence in your time of trouble. I will deliver you and bring you honor. I will satisfy you with a full life and with all that I do for you. For you will enjoy the fullness of my salvation!"

Psalm 91:1–16 (TPT)

Psalm 91:1 (TPT) says, "When you abide under the shadow of Shaddai, you are hidden." Can you just imagine that? Standing in the shadow of the *Almighty*? Knowing that nothing can harm you. What a wonderful feeling to know we are safe with Jesus! Shaddai is taken from the Hebrew root word with many expressive meanings. It can mean "God on the mountain," "God the Destroyer of Enemies," "God the Self-Sufficent One," "God the Nurturer of Babies," or "God Almighty." Moses, the lawgiver, is the author of this Psalm, yet every verse seems to breathe the unlimited grace and mercy of God.

Look at Job 39:28, where the same Hebrew word is used for an eagle passing the night on the high cliffs. Similarly, in Psalm 91:1 (NKJV), it is translated as "I endure through the night." You, my friends, can endure through the night, through the storms of life, when you are hidden in the shadows of our precious Savior. My prayer for you today is you will get to know Shaddai in a new way. That you will call upon His name and He will put you under the shadow of His wings!

One night as I was praying, I heard the Lord say, "Yeshua Hamashiach." I was uncertain of what I had heard or even what it meant, but I knew it was the voice of my sweet Jesus. These words were ringing in my soul, and I couldn't put it down. I just had to know what He was saying to me. As I researched the meaning of this word, I found the Hebrew meaning was "the Anointed One." Let's just wrap our minds around that: "The Anointed One" was speaking to me. He wanted me to know as I was praying in faith for people who were about to be healed or delivered. He was telling me who He was! He truly is "the Anointed One." Without "Yeshua Hamashiach" nothing can be healed, delivered, or cast out. We need Him in our lives just as we need the air we breathe. Jeremiah 29:13 (NKJV) tells us, "You will seek me and find me when you seek me with all your heart." I encourage you to seek Him and find Him. I pray you will go after His heart in a way you never have before! May we never grow weary in our walk with "Yeshua Hamashiach."

Jesus has many names, and these names describe His characteristics. Jehovah Rapha, our healer; Jehovah Jireh, our provider; Jehovah Nissi, our banner; or Jehovah Tsidkenu, our righteousness…these are just a few of the names of God. But we cannot truly understand these names until we experience Him through these characteristics. Do you know Him as healer or as your provider? His names give us insight into who our God truly is. He responds to our need. When you experience Him through your need, then you will truly know Him by that name. Take time to get to know the one true God and explore His character traits and the names that identify those traits. When you experience Him in these ways, you will have a deeper understanding of the many facets of God's character and the depth of His love for you. In what way do you need to learn who God is in your life?

Jesus, I want to know You as my healer. Come heal my body, mind, and soul. I confess I need You, Jehovah Rapha. Amen.

DAY 31:

"Healer of My Soul"

"Jesus traveled through all the towns and villages of that area, teaching in the synagogues and announcing the Good News about the Kingdom. And he healed every kind of disease and illness."

Matthew 9:35 (NLT)

I believe virtually everyone has some sort of spiritual wound that has affected us as adults. These wounds can be inflicted upon us by loved ones, teachers, friends, etc. Sometimes these wounds were not meant to harm us, but other times the wounds were quite intentional. The old saying, "Sticks and stones will break my bones, but words will never hurt me" is a lie straight from the pits of hell. Words cannot be taken back once they have been released. Often these words are spoken over us in our childhood. Let's give a few examples. A parent, when they are frustrated with a child who continually disobeys the parent's wishes, may say something like, "You're a worthless kid, and you'll probably end up in prison." Or maybe that parent would call their child a loser, no good, lazy, or stupid. Some of us had parents who used much more colorful language to get their point across. I know I did. I wonder, would a parent use this kind of language if they knew the things they said to or about their children could come to pass? Many women have set themselves up for a curse unknowingly; have you asked your husband how you look in an outfit? Has that same husband said something that makes you feel less than beautiful? Maybe he's even said something outright hurtful… "You look horrible in that outfit; it really makes you look fat!" Many women have asked that dreaded question to their husbands. The husband is probably just being honest and never intended to hurt you, but he did, nonetheless.

Many of us have endured word curses, things spoken over us that have the ability to come true. Sometimes we speak these words over ourselves…this is known as a self-fulfilling prophecy. We often joke around about these things, and if we knew these things could come to pass by us simply by speaking the words out into the atmosphere, then we would probably change the way we said things. How many times have you done something not quite how it should have been done, and you say something along the lines of "Oh, how stupid can I be? That was just dumb"? The examples that I have given may seem minor and not a big deal at all to most of us. But what if someone was told these things on a daily basis or even multiple times a day? This is psychological warfare at the extreme. If one is told something over and over, eventually the victim of those spoken words will begin to believe what is said about them.

Be careful of every word you speak so as not to ensnare yourself and others. Remember Proverbs 18:21 (NKJV) says, "Death and life are in the power of the tongue, And those who love it will eat its fruit." That, my friends, is a pretty clear word.

Now let's bring this same kind of thought pattern when a doctor gives you a negative report. Let's say the doctor has come in after some routine testing during your pregnancy and has delivered a message that your baby won't survive birth or that your baby will have a birth defect or even that there is a very strong likelihood that both you and the baby can die during birth. These are not uncommon examples. Many of you may have heard something similar. The question then becomes, what do you do with the diagnosis? Do you accept it? Or do you reject it and go against the doctor's recommendations? Do you go seek a second opinion? Or do you take the words spoken about your pregnancy to the Lord and ask Him what you should do? As a Christian you should never accept a negative report, even if true, and then you take it to God.

The first thing you should do in these cases is go to the Bible and find relevant scriptures that talk about your desired outcome. Then declare those scriptures…speak them out loud multiple times a day. Write them down on sticky notes and post them everywhere you go; post them on your bathroom mirror, on your computer screen, your office desk—put them everywhere! There is power in declarations and the spoken word. Jesus Himself said in Matthew 12:36–37 (NKJV), "But I say to you that for every idle word men may speak, they will give account of it in the day of judgment. For by your words you will be justified, and by your words you will be condemned." So speak words of life! When a doctor gives you a death sentence, say, "I shall not die but live and declare the works of the Lord." One of my favorites and a very common scripture used for healing is Isaiah 53:5 (NKJV): "But He was wounded for our transgressions, He was bruised for our iniquities; The chastisement for our peace was upon Him, And *by His stripes we are healed*" (emphasis mine). We are not *being* healed; we won't *be* healed—it says, "*We are healed*" already. These are the kinds of scriptures you speak over negative situations. Find what fits your circumstance and speak it out often. There was a school teacher named Everett Storms in Kitchener, Ontario, Canada, who made a detailed study of promises. During his twenty-seventh reading of the Bible, a task which took him a year and a half, Storms concluded that there were 8,810 promises in the Bible (7,487 of them being promises made by God to humankind).

All God's promises are yes and amen (see 2 Corinthians 1:20). Who knows how many promises are actually in the Bible? Yes, like Everett Storms, we can make an educated guess, but I'm not 100 percent certain we have a truly accurate number of all that God promises us. The point of all this is to say, find in the Bible what is relevant to you and work out your faith until it comes to pass. You see, in the promises of God, faith is a very big component. Just speaking the words out won't necessarily mean it will come to pass. The right words with the right beliefs and the right heart are critical to getting answers to prayer. The last example I will give you will be the story of the Roman centurion who had a sick servant in Matthew 8:5–13. The centurion's servant was so sick that he was expected to die at any moment. So the centurion had asked some elders to go to Jesus on his behalf to see if Jesus might be willing to heal his beloved servant. There's a lot of culturally sensitive stuff in this story if you sit down and study it out thoroughly, but I don't have time to get into all of that in this short devotional. So I'll skip to the end… Jesus ends up getting stopped by more representatives on the centurion's behalf…which went something like this: "Teacher, I have a message from you from my Roman friend. He says, 'Don't bother coming. I'm not worthy of You being under my roof. But if You simply say the word, I know my servant will be healed.'" Guess what? The Roman's servant was healed because of his master's great faith. Even Jesus marveled at the faith of the man who did not worship as other Jewish people of the day. Can you, too, level up your faith to where a spoken word brings healing for you or your loved one?

Jesus, help me to have faith to believe what You say is the final word. I need strength to declare and decree Your word and believe completely in You in all things. Jesus, I want You to be the healer of my soul. In Jesus' name. Amen.

DAY 32:

"Surrender"

I look up to the mountains and hills, longing for God's help. But then I realize that our true help and protection is only from the Lord, our Creator who made the heavens and the earth. He will guard and guide me, never letting me stumble or fall. God is my keeper; he will never forget nor ignore me. He will never slumber nor sleep; he is the Guardian-God for his people, Israel. Yahweh himself will watch over you; he's always at your side to shelter you safely in his presence. He's protecting you from all danger both day and night. He will keep you from every form of evil or calamity as he continuously watches over you. You will be guarded by God himself. You will be safe when you leave your home, and safely you will return. He will protect you now, and he'll protect you forevermore!

Psalm 121:1–8 (TPT)

Psalm 121 holds a precious place in my heart. This was a verse that our pastor would pray over one of my sons who was very sick as a child. The pastor would come by weekly or so often to check on him, and I would hear him reciting this verse almost every time he came. I did not have the relationship with Jesus I have now, so in hearing it, I did not know the power and the meaning behind it. Now, my son is a grown man, and I still read this verse in my Bible and see his little face. His name is written on this Bible verse in my Bible. It's such a beautiful reminder of how much we are loved by Jesus, and as I look up, I truly know where my help came from! It's a great reminder that He is fighting my battles even when I have no fight left.

During my prayer time one day, I had a tremendous urging from the Lord that Jesus is in the process of building an army for battle! Because of this, the atmosphere is changing! Can you feel it? So, you might be asking yourself, *What do I need to do to be part of His army?* First and foremost, you must be seeking His face and not His hand! His presence, His guidance, and His voice are what we should actively be looking for and listening to. Your action step, and mine, is to daily put on the full armor of God as found in Ephesians 6:10–18. Are you beginning to catch the militaristic theme here? Army…battle… surrender; make no mistake about it, we are at war.

Surrender: As I lift my hands to Jesus to surrender, one might ask, "What does that look like?" I have many people ask me this question. I simply say, "Surrender is an act of laying everything you are trying to carry on the altar." Sometimes, the problem is not laying them down but rather picking them up again.

We try to control the situation, and God is simply saying, "Give it to Me." As we hold onto what God is wanting to heal or whatever the issue may be, He will not take it from us; we must surrender it all to Him.

I tell people it's like taking that situation that no man or woman can fix and handing it over to Jesus and saying, "Lord, I can't, but I know *You* can, and You will do whatever is best for me in the situation. I know God is still God, and God is still good, and I give Him all the *glory*, no matter the outcome." God is such a gentleman. He will not force Himself on us, so this is where we must trust Him completely with every situation. He already won the battle on the cross, so all we have to do is lay it down and trust Him.

I love Psalm 121. He is my help in times of trouble, and I choose to surrender to His will and His ways. I pray you will also surrender to Him. That, my friends, is enough for me.

Oh, how He loves us! Matthew 6:33 (NKJV) comes to mind: "But seek first the kingdom of God and His righteousness, and all things shall be added to you." Are you seeking His kingdom? Are you chasing after Jesus?

Jesus, thank You for giving me Your Word and for helping me in times of trouble. Help me to surrender anything I am holding onto and to trust You in all things. In Jesus' name. Amen.

DAY 33:

"He Cares for You"

"Give all your worries and cares to God, for he cares about you."

1 Peter 5:7 (NLT)

You are not forgotten! Let that sink in a minute. The God of the universe cares about you, and He has not left you nor forgotten about you. The Almighty God, who keeps the planets in their orbits, is aware, at the same time, of the sparrow that falls to the ground. In Luke 12:4–7, Jesus talks about how five sparrows are sold for a measly two copper coins, yet God is aware of each of them. And it goes on to say, "Are you not worth more than many sparrows?" His eyes are on you even now as you read this devotion.

You may be feeling unnoticed by God right now. You might wonder if He even cares about your troubles. He is God, after all; He does have bigger problems and issues to deal with than the pain you're going through. These might be some of your thoughts during this time in your life. Today's verse makes it clear that this is not the case at all…those thoughts are just more of the same from the enemy; they're all lies! Are you feeling right now like no one can understand your pain? Or that no one understands the sorrow you are dealing with? It's interesting how Satan plays mind games with us. He wants us to feel all alone so he can isolate us. When we feel alone and we isolate ourselves from others, we are much more vulnerable to his attacks.

Let's look at today's verse in The Passion Translation, "Pour out all your worries and stress upon him and leave them there, for He always tenderly cares for you." Does that sound like a God who has forgotten about His creation? He cares so much about you that He wants you to give Him all your worries, all your stress, and all your pain. He loves you with an everlasting love. See Jeremiah 31:3. He will even send people into our lives who have been through the very things we are going through right now. If we only allow Him access to our pain, He will begin the process of healing through a variety of means. It could be through others, or He could use a book or even a song. The point is God knows exactly what we need when we need it.

Think about how Jesus was constantly instructing His disciples on how much the Father cares for them. Jesus told them His Father cared even about the birds being fed. He went on the tell them that if He cares about the birds of the air, how much more will He see to the needs of His children? Satan's goal is to get you to question or doubt how much God cares for you. All you have to do is look to the cross for the answer of how much God loves you.

Paul said, "If God spared not His own Son but delivered Him up for us all, how much more shall He not freely give us all things?" Or maybe John put it even better in the most memorized Bible verse of all time (John 3:16, NKJV), "For God so loved the world that He gave His only begotten Son, that whoever believes in Him should not perish but have everlasting life."

Take some time today to meditate on God's love for you. Learn about how much He cares for you. Trust in God's Word, not in Satan's lies. When you begin to feel weak and start feeling sorry for yourself, remember…He cares for you! Will you trust your Father in heaven with all your hurts, with all your pain, and with all your worries?

Heavenly Father, I want to feel Your love. I want to know You care about me like Your Word

says You do. Come and help me as I sit with You to find this love and mercy You have for me.

In Jesus' name. Amen.

DAY 34:

"The Blood Sets Us Free"

"He himself carried our sins in his body on the cross so that we would be dead to sin and live for righteousness. Our instant healing flowed from his wounding."

1 Peter 2:24 (TPT)

"There is power, power wonderworking power in blood of the Lamb." These words from an old gospel hymn speak volumes. The words from today's verse are quoted by Peter from the Old Testament in Isaiah 53:5, another well-known Bible verse. In case you are not familiar with the verse from Isaiah, it says, "But He was wounded for our transgressions, He was bruised for our iniquities; The chastisement for our peace was upon Him, And by His stripes we are healed." The blood is what sets us free. The blood is enough.

Jesus died on a cross for all of humanity. Even for those we think aren't worthy. Yet the truth is we ourselves are not worthy of the gift of His blood, which washes us free from all our sins. Not even the most righteous person without the blood is worthy of entry into the kingdom of heaven. It's the blood that separates Christianity from every other religion. It's the blood that cleanses us from our sin.

This is the new covenant we have through Jesus Christ. But this dates to even the first temple. The high priest, once per year, would offer a sacrifice for the people of the tribes of Israel. He would place the sins and the blood of the sacrifice onto the head of the scapegoat sending it off into the wilderness of an uninhabited land. The prophet Isaiah foretold the atonement once and for all in Isaiah 53:5. Isaiah was making it clear that there would no longer be the necessity of an annual sacrifice. The coming sacrifice would be sufficient to end all sacrifices. Jesus' blood is enough! In fact, one drop of His blood would have been enough to save all humanity. And He would have sacrificed Himself if it were for just you! He died for all of us, but He would have died for one of us.

There is no sin He can't forgive. There is no sin that He did not bear on the cross. There is no person that He won't forgive if only they believe in the greatest sacrifice of all. Can you imagine the load that Jesus bore on the cross for us? The weight of every sin for every person who has ever lived and ever will live. The weight of every sickness and disease. The weight of every wound ever afflicted upon us. My mind cannot comprehend the depth of His love for us to do such a thing. He died even for the least of us.

The thought I can't seem to get past is that one drop of His blood was enough. Yet He suffered an incredible beating to the point where His face was unrecognizable. He endured the nails being driven into His wrists and feet. He suffered the suffocation from the weight of His own body. Not only the physical pain and suffering, but He also bore the spiritual pain of sin even though He Himself was sinless. How could someone who was sinless for all thirty-three years of His life bear every sin that has ever been committed?

He bore all those sins for you, for me, and for our loved ones who have gone on ahead of us. Without Jesus' blood, you would not have the opportunity to see your baby again. It's only by His blood that we have the extraordinary opportunity to experience eternal life. Jesus said in John 14:6 (NKJV), "I am the way, the truth, and the life. No one comes to the Father except through Me." There is no other way…the blood is enough.

His blood covers not only every sin but every wound. When it says we are healed by His stripes, it is saying that you are healed because Jesus gave His body for you. He was broken so that you don't have to be. He was bruised, He was crushed, and He was pierced so we wouldn't have to be. While we can take this to mean only healing of our broken bodies, I believe He also wants to heal us from every place of pain in our life. He never meant for us to suffer. So give it all to Him, and invite Him into every wound. What wound in your life are you not allowing Jesus to heal?

Jesus, thank You for going to the cross for me and shedding Your blood so one day I can be with You in heaven. I am eternally grateful. In Jesus' mighty name. Amen.

DAY 35:

"The Lord of Restoration"

"'I will give you back your health and heal your wounds,' says the Lord. 'For you are called an outcast—'Jerusalem for whom no one cares.'"

Jeremiah 30:17 (NLT)

Have you experienced a holiday without your loved one? The first holiday without them is tortuous at best! Whether you have lost a baby, a child, a brother or sister, a parent, or a spouse, it doesn't really matter whom you may have lost if you were close to that person having a deep connection to someone that is no longer with you. The holidays and special occasions can be especially rough for those of us who have lost someone close to us. If you can identify with this, then I know you know how painful these events can be.

It's difficult for anybody who has experienced loss, but I believe it's even more so for mothers who have lost a baby. Your mind immediately turns to thoughts of what they would be like or if they would enjoy a certain tradition or what kind of toys they would want. A myriad of thoughts come rushing in on these occasions for Momma. Meanwhile, she tries to put on a brave face for all the world to see, while on the inside she is crushed emotionally and spiritually. This is how a mother can cope with this particular season in life when all the world around her is celebrating while she is heartbroken. It makes me think of the commercials for the pharmaceutical products for depression. The lady is going through deep depression, but she holds up this cardboard smiley face on a stick and places it over her face. Many mothers feel just like this…and likely some daddies too.

While never pleasant, these seasons are a time of crushing. God will use the crushing to produce new wine in your life, and along with the new wine, a new wineskin is needed (see Matthew 9:16–17). You see new wine will ruin the old wineskins. Fermented wine was placed into new wineskins to allow for the natural expansion process of the wine; the new wineskin expands with the growth from the new wine. As Christians we are taken from glory to glory or one realm to a new realm. When we first come to Christ, our perspectives can't line up with the new life we are supposed to live. The crushing will cause us to gain a new perspective on our old life. This is never a pleasant process, but it always causes us to grow if we can properly deal with the crushing and not try to fit our new perspectives into our old lifestyle or thought processes.

Another way to look at it is the example of the refining process. The refiner superheats the molten gold or silver, and then the impurities in the metal ore begin to surface where the impurities are skimmed off the surface and the process starts over again until the desired level of purity is achieved. This super-heating process is similar to the crushing process of making wine from ripe fruit. God seeks for us to be pure and holy, as He is pure and holy. But as long as we are living and thinking in the old flesh, we can't achieve the desired level of purity He seeks for us. During the process of refining or crushing, you likely will think this is one cruel joke. God doesn't create the crushing/refining, but He will use it to obtain the purity needed for the next level in our walk with Him.

Acts 16:31 says that if we believe on the Lord Jesus Christ, then we will be saved and our whole household. We each are responsible for our own walk with Jesus, but if we receive salvation, then everyone under our covering will hear the gospel message and will be predisposed to receive Him. And in Hebrews 1:14 it talks about how angels are ministering spirits that are sent forth from the throne of God to minister to those who will inherit salvation. Did you catch the word "will"? He's not sending these angels to those who already have salvation but to those who *will* receive salvation. So let's major on the majors and remember the ultimate hope we have in Jesus. We will see our loved ones again if we trust in His ways and cooperate with His processes for healing and growth in our life. Jesus is our hope! Are you ready to receive the new wine in your life?

Jesus, I pray You give me grace as I try to handle what is ahead of me during this time in my life. Give me strength as I try to cry my way this holiday and help me rest knowing You will give me new wine for this season of my life. In Jesus' name. Amen.

DAY 36:

"Run to Him"

Are you weary, carrying a heavy burden? Come to me. I will refresh your life, for I am your oasis. Simply join your life with mine. Learn my ways and you'll discover that I'm gentle, humble, easy to please. You will find refreshment and rest in me. For all that I require of you will be pleasant and easy to bear.

Matthew 11:28–30 (TPT)

The loss of an infant or a baby will cause you to feel weary. I believe it's also fair to say this creates a heavy burden. It's so hard to try to figure this all out. Whether your loss has just happened or occurred many years ago, the pain can be just as fresh as the day your baby passed on to be with the Lord. Sometimes even the simple memory of this loss will send even a well-stable mother into a bit of tailspin.

The pain is almost unbearable at times! Personally, I started this journey to healing by suppressing the emotions and tried to deal with the pain on my own. I was angry and heartbroken, and the last thing I wanted to do was to talk about it with others. You may or may not be in the same place I was when I lost my son. We all handle pain and loss differently, and there is a right and wrong way to deal with that pain. Holding onto the pain and not expressing how you are feeling with those who want to help is not the right way to deal with the hurt. The good news is God is waiting for you to release that burden. He wants to carry your pain and your hurt. Do not become hard-hearted and fail to let Him into the wound.

Worshipping the King of kings and Lord of lords, your Creator, is the beginning of healing and deliverance from the pain. Invite Him into the wound and hand over the reigns to Him. He is waiting for you to release it to Him. In the New King James Version in Matthew 11:29, it says to "take my yoke upon you." A yoke was an implement placed upon cattle or slaves to bear a burden. Jesus was basically saying, "Let Me have the reigns of your life, and I will guide you to the work I have for you." He has a purpose and plan for you, but you cannot get within His plan until you let go of the burden you are trying to carry alone. The burden you are trying to carry on your own is not from God. You must release that burden, and Jesus will exchange it for the load you are designed to carry…His burden is a much easier load because He is carrying most of the weight. We just have to cooperate with Him and leave our burdens on the altar.

God is seeking true worshipers! Wrap your mind around that…God Almighty is seeking "true" worshipers (John 4:23)! God is Spirit, and those who worship Him *must* worship in the spirit and truth (John 4:24)! Are you a true worshiper? Do you worship our precious Jesus in the spirit? Do you really know what that looks like? It's letting go of yourself and releasing all your spirit and soul to Jesus! It's giving Him *all* of *you*! All the hidden places that are within you…He gets them *all*! I would encourage you today to seek Him like never before. Seek "Him" while "He" may be found (Isaiah 55:6). Oh, my friends, He is worthy of all our true praise and worship!

When we are able to release our burdens unto Him, it's almost like releasing praise to Him. How? Because it says to God, "I can't bear the weight of this mess, but I know You can." He loves to respond to our needs; He loves to be needed. When we ask Him to get involved with our burdens, He responds with kindness and love and guides us into a still, quiet place. He delights in you…in Psalm 149:4 (NKJV), it says, "The Lord takes pleasure in His people." If He takes pleasure in you, why would He seek to keep you in pain? He doesn't want you to stay in a place of woundedness. He wants you whole and healed. Are you still holding onto your pain, or have you released it to Him?

Jesus, help me release all my hurts and pains to You. Help me see You in all the mess that's around me right now. You are my safe place, and I need You. In Jesus' name. Amen.

DAY 37:

"Right Now I Need a Little Hope"

"So you shall serve the Lord your God, and He will bless your bread and your water. And I will take sickness away from the midst of you. No one shall suffer miscarriage or be barren in your land; I will fulfill the number of your days."

Exodus 23:25–26 (NKJV)

Miscarriage is every bit as tragic as losing a child at birth. For those who have had a miscarriage, there is a sense of dread in trying to have another baby. Let's face it—when you do miscarry, most people really have no idea how to console you. Their words are empty at best and can be downright hurtful. It's not because they mean to hurt you; it's just that the devil will use anybody to bring a spoken curse over your life. Words like… "You weren't very far along; it really wasn't a baby anyway," or "It's okay; you'll get pregnant again," or some other word similar to these. And for those who have had multiple miscarriages, it's even more painful with each loss.

I had a pastor friend who, he and his wife, lost seven babies due to miscarriage. He told me that seemingly every time they got a little hope the devil would swoop in and take it all away. They told me that the most painful words came from family and members of his church family. People would try to comfort them, but most could not sympathize. He said, "I don't want sympathy; I just want someone to recognize our loss." In the entryway of their home are found seven empty picture frames with the names of the babies that never took a breath here on earth. It was important to them to name their babies who were lost due to miscarriage. It gave them a sense of identity to their children that never made it past the womb.

For those who haven't lost a baby to miscarriage, I would simply encourage you to empathize with those who have. Recognize the loss of those babies and don't try to comfort the parents. Simply be there for them and give them a shoulder to cry on. They simply want someone to legitimize their loss. Be very guarded with your words. Our words have the power to bring life or death. It may not be physical death that you bring, but you could speak death to these parents' hopes and dreams. My grandma once told me, "If you don't know what to say to someone, don't say anything at all." Speak only words that will bring life to a difficult situation.

For those of you who have lost a baby due to miscarriage, just know this…we have a comforter in

Jesus Christ. He knows your pain and bore it on the cross. He can sympathize with you; take all your hurts, cares, and fears to Him. Trust His plan for your life. His ways are not our ways (see Isaiah 55:8–9). I encourage you to dig into Scripture and prayer. The Lord tells us to seek Him with our whole heart.

There is hope on the other side of brokenness. Remember my pastor friend? He and his wife did end up having a precious little boy, and, next to Jesus, he was their world. May the Lord bless you with a child of your own, or you may get to choose your child through adoption, or maybe you decide to love someone else's child and be a second mommy or daddy to them. The impact you can have on a child's life, whether your own or not, is priceless. Never forget who you are in Christ, and know that you are not less than because you had a miscarriage. You will never forget the baby that you should have carried to term and birthed. So name that baby and celebrate him or her. They are watching from heaven and can't wait to see you when your time on earth is done.

There's an old Christian hymn that has lyrics that say, "My hope is built on nothing less than Jesus' blood and righteousness." Do you have hope? What is your hope built upon?

Jesus, help me with my unbelief that I can and will carry a baby one day. Your plans are higher than mine, and I need You to lead me down the path I should go. In Jesus' name.

Amen.

DAY 38:

"Who Touched Me?"

Now a certain woman had a flow of blood for twelve years, and had suffered many things from many physicians. She had spent all that she had and was no better, but rather grew worse. When she heard about Jesus, she came behind Him in the crowd and touched His garment. For she said, "If only I may touch His clothes, I shall be made well." Immediately the fountain of her blood was dried up, and she felt in her body that she was healed of the affliction. And Jesus, immediately knowing in Himself that power had gone out of Him, turned around in the crowd and said, "Who touched My clothes?" But His disciples said to Him, "You see the multitude thronging You, and You say, 'Who touched Me?'" And He looked around to see her who had done this thing. But the woman, fearing and trembling, knowing what had happened to her, came and fell down before Him and told Him the whole truth. And He said to her, "Daughter, your faith has made you well. Go in peace and be healed of your affliction."

Mark 5:25–34 (NKJV)]

When you read this passage, do you wonder why the woman wanted to touch Jesus? I believe she knew that with just one touch from Him her whole life would change forever! As we are walking through trials and pains of this life, we should strive to be like this woman, push through all the difficulties, and reach out for Jesus. He can and will change our lives forever if we push into Him and invite Him into our difficulties.

After the death of my first son, Brandon, I was so sure my life was over as I knew it, and it actually was. The life I had planned was gone in an instant when Brandon died. But Jesus had bigger and better plans for my life. This is where my rainbow baby came in. I wanted so desperately to have a family. I wanted a baby more than anything. The loss of my son was such a deep pain, but I just knew having another child would take away all this pain, but I was wrong. I thought, deep in my heart, that having another child would somehow minimize the loss of Brandon. But it didn't minimize the loss at all. Even now I still remember Brandon's birthday and long for the life that could have been. I wonder what kind of man he would have grown up to be. Would I have had more grandchildren through him too?

It wasn't necessarily another child I needed; Jesus was what I needed. Fortunately, I finally had my bundle of joy, and boy, was he everything I ever wanted and more. I thought to myself now the pain would go away, but it did not. I was much like Mary in Luke 2:19 (NKJV), which says, "But Mary kept all these things and pondered them in her heart." This was after the shepherds had visited her and the newborn Jesus. The words "pondered them in her heart" indicate that Mary did not fully understand everything she was experiencing and learning about her son.

Like Mary, I kept the pain deep in my heart as I loved and nurtured my "rainbow baby." I so desperately was searching for healing from the loss of Brandon, and I thought my new son would bring healing. But you see, I needed to find Jesus and touch the hem of His garment so I could be made whole in Him so I could be the mother He called me to be.

God blessed me in ways I never dreamed possible through my "rainbow baby" as I got the most precious daughter in love and granddaughter. Now as I watch my granddaughter laugh and play, I see so much of her daddy in her. That personality is as big as life, like her daddy. What a blessing!

Have you reached out for Jesus in your pain?

Jesus, the pain is real. I need a little hope right now. Let me see You in this storm. Let me run to You and grab the hem of Your garment so I may be healed. In Jesus' mighty name. Amen.

DAY 39:

"Restore Me"

"O Lord, by these things men live, And in all these is the life of my spirit; Restore me to health and let me live!"

Isaiah 38:16 (AMP)

Your special day has finally arrived; you're excited beyond belief awaiting to meet your baby for the very first time. Your bags are packed, and your husband is so nervous trying to make everything perfect for you and your new bundle of joy. Everything is going perfectly normal. You get to the labor and delivery room and begin to settle in for the duration. While you're in great pain and discomfort, the excitement is overwhelming. Things are progressing as routine as any normal labor and delivery.

Suddenly things shift, and there is a tremendous amount of activity, and the atmosphere changes to a sense of urgency. The nurses are trying to reassure you and Daddy, but there is a feeling that something has changed and the birth is no longer normal. The baby is at risk suddenly with a faint heartbeat and is taking very few breaths. The doctor and nurses are fighting for the baby's life, but it turns out to be all for naught. The baby was unable to survive the birth. It could have been due to an assignable cause, or the baby could have died for seemingly no reason at all. The excitement of giving birth gives way to extreme grief and brokenness. Life changes immediately, and there is no comfort, and you're wondering how to go on with life.

Restoration is the last thing on your mind in this moment. There is naturally the process of going through the cycle of grief and mourning. Sometimes this doesn't really begin until after the funeral arrangements have been made and the funeral is over. When all the people who have said they would be there for you disappear to go on with their own lives. It's when you are all alone and faced with beginning life again that you have to figure out how to go about life the way it used to be. But your life will never be the same again. You are faced with a proverbial fork in the road; one road leads to life with depression, sadness, and a dark cloud that never really goes away, but the second fork will walk you through the pain of your loss, ultimately leading to healing. Unconsciously you are faced with this fork in the road. No one chooses to embark on a life of deep depression and sadness…it just happens that way. You must intentionally choose the other path that leads to healing.

To choose the healing path, you will be forced to deal with your grief in a healthy way, looking inwardly and inviting God into the pain, asking Him to restore you back to life. The fact is other people in your family are depending on you to choose the path to healing. Your husband, your parents, and possibly other children need you in their lives. While you have changed because of your loss, these family members only know you the way you used to be. This is where you must ask God to restore you again, and your responsibility is to seek Him first. He doesn't want you to go through life in pain. He wants to use your grief to empower you so you can help someone else. You must go deeper into your intimacy with the Father…reading His Word, trying to find peace for your life, staying in a state of prayer and communication with your Heavenly Father, and staying connected with like-minded friends. Do not isolate yourself thinking you can get through this on your own. When you find yourself in a state of deep pain, reach out to others to help you through this phase.

When you turn to Jesus and invite Him into your pain, you will be able to eventually return to life once again. It may not seem possible right now—just keep putting one foot in front of the other and keep moving forward. There is an old gospel hymn by Patsy Cline called "One Day at a Time"; some of the lyrics include: "I'm only human, I'm just a woman, help be believe in what I could be, and all that I am, Oh show me the stairway that I have to climb, Lord, for my sake, teach me to take One day at a time." Are you ready for Jesus to restore you back to life?

Lord, I need You. I need Your help because I can't do this on my own. Come, Jesus, into all the broken places in my heart and restore me. In Jesus' name. Amen.

DAY 40:

"Shattered"

"He heals the wounds of every shattered heart."

Psalm 147:3 (TPT)

Divorce is ugly. We grow up and get a family and think life will be great, but sometimes we get a curve ball thrown in there. Divorce comes and shatters our hearts and our children's hearts. These babies we prayed for are now thrown from home to home, holidays here and holidays there…yes, we keep going, but not much is really thought of how the children are truly feeling. Then they grow up to be broken adults even though we thought we did so well in raising them. You see, our shattered and broken hearts can only be healed by our Savior. We need Him more than we need the air we breathe. Our children need Him. All of creation yearns for Him.

When the outcome isn't what I hoped for, I will still declare the Lord is good. No one goes into marriage with the idea that it will end in divorce. In essence, it is a loss of hopes and dreams built upon a life together. When the marriage ends, it is certainly a loss for the couple, but the impact upon children can be immeasurable. Children have divided loyalties and sometimes are forced to choose between Mom or Dad. There is always a loser in a divorce; most of the time, the ones who really lose are the children.

And sometimes, through that broken marriage, you will remarry, and God will give you another little life to love, as He did me. My baby will always be my baby no matter how old he gets. He now has a family of his own with a beautiful, godly wife and two of my most precious granddaughters. You see, through my shattered heart, He brought some of the best gifts in my life. I am so grateful for my family. Sometimes, I sit back and say, "Jesus, this old broken bag of bones…You restored and gave me life and life more abundantly!"

God has blessed me with five wonderful sons, and He has forgiven me for all my wrongs. He gave me new life in Him, but still my children had areas in their lives that Jesus had to heal. There is always healing on the other side of brokenness through Jesus Christ. Children must be nurtured through the wounds that the parents place in them. The parents definitely have a role to play in helping the children through the wounds they placed in them. But ultimately, it's the child's responsibility to find their own way to Jesus. He is where their help comes from (Psalm 121:1). It's the parents' role to ensure the child is introduced to Jesus and to provide a healthy home life…the parents must demonstrate Christ-like behavior in all they do.

The shattered lives that come from divorce can be repaired and restored into a beautiful mosaic if Christ is at the center. Jesus is the way, the truth, and the life. No one comes to the Father except through Him (John 14:6). There is an old saying that says, "Time heals all wounds." That saying is a lie straight from Satan. Time does not heal all wounds; Jesus does! Jesus came to take away our pain, shame, guilt, and wounds. So turn to Jesus, my friends, whether you are the mom, dad, or child. Jesus will bring healing to all of the bitterness and unforgiveness. When we place our trust in Him, rest assured He will lead us through all the trials and snares of divorce. Fear not—one day you will learn to love and trust again. Have you trusted Jesus with all your wounds?

Jesus, I am so grateful You took my shattered heart and restored more than I could even imagine. Thank You for loving me so well. In Jesus' mighty name. Amen.

DAY 41:

"All Things Possible"

"Jesus looked at them and replied, 'With people it is impossible, but not with God—God makes all things possible!'"

Mark 10:27 (TPT)

Imagine waking up to a normal day, going through a normal routine, when you receive a phone call from the person watching your children while you are working. I remember this day like it was yesterday. My youngest brother was babysitting my children that day, and he called me at work frantically, telling me that one of my sons was having some extreme behavior. To make a long story short, I'll say my son was rushed to the hospital and was put under sedation for an MRI. The doctors didn't seem to know what was wrong until they ran a brain scan, which seemed to take an eternity. It was after this lengthy scan that I was told my son had a massive brain tumor.

Little did I know that morning when I went into work that my life was about to take a drastic shift. My son was rushed to surgery about two hours away from where we lived. I was told he had about a fifty-fifty chance of surviving the surgery and that they really didn't know what he would be like if he did survive. We really had no idea of what the outcome would be. At this point, I became completely numb. I couldn't eat, I couldn't sleep, and I couldn't even pray. I was fortunate to have a fantastic prayer circle that filled the gap on behalf of me and my family. There was another family that had brought their daughter in for the same surgery at the same time as my son. Two children went back, but only one survived. Fortunately, my son lived through the surgery, but surviving the surgery was only the beginning of a long, arduous journey.

Praying for someone is like wrapping them in a blanket of God's love. My prayer team prayed my family and me through one of the most difficult times of my life. While I was stressed and worried and unable to connect with God on my own. God used these friends to guide me through each step. My son had a large portion of his brain removed. Needless to say, the prognosis of a normal life looked impossible at the time. But God led me through every step—what doctors to see, how to handle behavioral issues, and how to deal with the unknown were all daily decisions that had to be made. Through all this, I had to quit my job to be by his side, so I had to turn every decision over to God. Meanwhile, a good friend from our church gave my son a little wooden cross with Mark 10:27 written on it when he had the brain tumor removed. This would become his source of strength and hope through the years.

Prayer was the key that opened the door to healing and a relatively normal life for my son. He is now well into his thirties, about to complete his third year of Bible college, and has a goal of becoming a pastor for special needs children. On the side he builds websites to earn extra income. He has also written two books on his own. Don't tell me God doesn't answer prayers. Don't tell me God doesn't do the impossible today. My God is the God of miracles, and my son is definitely a miracle. The things he has had to overcome would astound you. He continues to overcome and fight against the odds. All his faith is in Jesus Christ. The medical world gave him little odds of even living a normal life. I say he's lived an extraordinary life.

The following quote from Corrie Tenboom really sums up how, as a family, we were able to overcome all the obstacles the enemy put in our path: "The wonderful thing about praying is that you leave a world of not being able to do something and enter God's realm where everything is possible. He specializes in the impossible. Nothing is too great for His almighty power. Nothing is too small for His love." In short, the impossible is possible with God…I would even go so far as to say the impossible is probable with God. When things look impossible is when He goes to work. Do you have faith for the impossible in your life?

Jesus, help me feel You wrap Your arms around my family and me as I travel down this unknown road that lies ahead of me. I trust You with the impossible. In Jesus' name. Amen.

DAY 42:

"Wings of Healing"

"But for you who fear my name, the Sun of Righteousness will rise with healing in his wings. And you will go free, leaping with joy like calves let out to pasture."

Malachi 4:2 (NLT)

I have talked about my being diagnosed with a terminal illness earlier in these devotions. After going through a couple of years of a variety of different treatments with little to no success, I was sitting in my doctor's office, and he looked me in the eye and said, "I want you to get a dog." We looked at him with a curious look on our face. We were just recently dog-free, and we had no plans to get another dog. He told me, "A dog will give you something to take care of and will take your mind off your illness. A dog will also give you something to fight for." My husband and I looked at each other, and we thought to ourselves, *This guy must be crazy...he's one of the top experts in the world for this disease, and instead of recommending some novel, new treatment option, he tells us to go get a dog.*

This advice turned out to be exactly what we needed. I grew up with boxers, and they've always been my favorite breed of dog! We started looking for a boxer locally. We had a recommendation from someone who told us about a breeder less than an hour's drive from us. The problem was I was so sick that I couldn't travel far at all. I spoke with the breeder, and she told me they had one puppy left from a recent litter. He had already been to three other homes, and they all brought him back. The last home he was in wanted to keep him. This was a pastor who came from another state and took him home with them over the weekend. They brought him back and told the breeder, who was a woman's pastor, "We love him already, but he belongs to someone else."

The breeder was dumbfounded why people kept bringing him back...the breeder's husband thought he was the pick of the litter, and he really wanted to keep him. But circumstances just wouldn't let them keep the pup. She happened to be in our town, and she asked if she could drop by. She got to our house and had the puppy with her. She placed him in my lap, and it was a done deal. I was head over tail in love with him. To make a long story a little shorter—that is how Malachi came into my life!

Malachi means a messenger from God. We wanted a biblical name, but we couldn't find a masculine name we really liked for a dog. We ended up deciding on the name Malachi. He has certainly lived up to his name. And I loved him from the start...my sons might even say I love him more than I love them.

That's not true, of course, but he certainly is a huge part of my life. He truly was sent by God, and he was meant for us from the beginning.

God knows exactly what we need and when we need it. He knows every little thing about us, even things we may not share with others. Sometimes the packaging doesn't look like we think it should look like. Somehow God intricately weaves things into our lives that may be insignificant to someone else. But that seemingly insignificant thing ends up changing our life. We weren't looking for a dog, and I didn't expect him to be such a huge part of my life and my healing. He's been through so much with me, and he has loved me unconditionally. In this sense, Malachi has given me a small glimpse into the love of God. There is nothing I could do to lose Malachi's love. Likewise, God loves me unconditionally too! He loved me so much that He sent a dog to walk with me on the path to healing. I'm not totally healed yet, but the last nine years with this dog have been something I could never part with. I know one day I will get my healing…either on this side of heaven or the other. I also know that one day Malachi will have to take that walk across the rainbow bridge. But I am so thankful God sent me His messenger to show me how much He loves me.

Don't expect God to move in the way you think He should. Be open to God's surprises in your life and watch what He does with it. Has God sent a surprise into your life?

Jesus, thank You for entrusting me with one of Your loving creatures that I get to love on and walk with through my healing. I needed him much more than he needed me. Malachi has allowed me to see the love of my Savior in his big brown eyes. I know You used him as a mighty tool for my healing, and I am eternally grateful. Malachi is a true messenger from God. In Jesus' name. Amen.

DAY 43:

"I Will Arise"

Now it happened on another Sabbath, also, that He entered the synagogue and taught. And a man was there whose right hand was withered. So the scribes and Pharisees watched Him closely, whether He would heal on the Sabbath, that they might find an accusation against Him. But He knew their thoughts, and said to the man who had the withered hand, "Arise and stand here." And he arose and stood. Then Jesus said to them, "I will ask you one thing: Is it lawful on the Sabbath to do good or to do evil, to save life or to destroy?" And when He had looked around at them all, He said to the man, "Stretch out your hand." And he did so, and his hand was restored as whole as the other. But they were filled with rage, and discussed with one another what they might do to Jesus.

Luke 6:6–11 (NKJV)

Horatio Spafford knew something about life's unexpected challenges. He was a successful attorney and real estate investor who lost a fortune in the great Chicago fire of 1871. Around the same time, his beloved four-year-old son died of scarlet fever.

Thinking a vacation would do his family some good, he sent his wife and four daughters on a ship to England, planning to join them after he finished some pressing business at home. However, while crossing the Atlantic Ocean, the ship was involved in a terrible collision and sunk. More than 200 people lost their lives, including all four of Horatio Spafford's precious daughters. His wife, Anna, survived the tragedy. Upon arriving in England, she sent a telegram to her husband that began: "Saved alone. What shall I do?"

Horatio immediately set sail for England. At one point during his voyage, the captain of the ship, aware of the tragedy that had struck the Spafford family, summoned Horatio to tell him that they were now passing over the spot where the shipwreck had occurred.[10]

As Horatio thought about his daughters, words of comfort and hope filled his heart and mind. He wrote them down, and they have since become a well-beloved hymn:

When peace like a river, attendeth my way,

When sorrows like sea billows roll—

Whatever my lot, thou hast taught me to know

It is well, it is well with my soul.[11]

---

10 See Randy Petersen, *Be Still My Soul: The Inspiring Stories behind 175 of the Most-Loved Hymns* (1973), 153.
11 See Randy Petersen, *Be Still My Soul*, 153.

No matter what the outcome of my situation…it is well with my soul. That is a tough statement, but I feel it deep with me. No matter what I go through or what gets thrown at me, I know God is and will always be right there with me. It says in Deuteronomy 31:6 (NKJV), "Be strong and of good courage, do not fear nor be afraid of them; for the Lord your God, He is the One who goes with you. He will not leave you nor forsake you."

Life has not exactly handled me roses. My road has been long and very hard. But Jesus has walked with me through it all as a friend. The death of a child is so difficult, but there is hope for healing in this. The world can be a brutal place that seeks to destroy everyone who tries to stop the rise of evil or even those who partner with Jesus. But God's Word is very clear. There are numerous stories of those who overcame the brutality of this world. But one of my favorite verses is found in the final book of the Bible, Revelation. "He who has an ear, let him hear what the Spirit says to the churches. To him who overcomes I will give to eat from the tree of life, which is in the midst of the Paradise of God" (Revelation 2:7, NKJV). Now that is a promise. I believe we can all hold onto with everything within us. Bible heroes are one thing, but more recent stories like that of Horatio Spafford seem a little more relevant to us. How can one write a beautiful hymn like "It Is Well with My Soul" after experiencing such great loss? The secret is no secret at all. It is putting all your trust and all your faith in someone greater; Jesus is the healer of our soul and will bring you His perfect peace in any circumstance. Are you ready to rise above your circumstance?

Jesus, my life has not been easy, and I struggle trying to find my way many times, but I pray I can say, "It is well with my soul." In Jesus' name. Amen.

DAY 44:

"He Is Good"

Let all that I am praise the Lord; with my whole heart, I will praise his holy name. Let all that I am praise the Lord; may I never forget the good things he does for me. He forgives all my sins and heals all my diseases. He redeems me from death and crowns me with love and tender mercies. He fills my life with good things. My youth is renewed like the eagle's!

Psalm 103:1–5 (NLT)

Life seems to throw us a curve ball when we least expect it. Marriage, getting pregnant, then preparing to bring home a baby! These are all such exciting times, but what if things don't turn out the way you planned them? It rarely does. I would tell you even in the times when things seem to go beyond our control, we serve a God who is always in control, and He will give us strength for the journey. You just have to lean into His Word and trust the process. That seems easy for me to say but very difficult to put into practice, especially if you don't have a relationship with Him.

So let's start here…to know Him, really know Him, you must read His Word. I am in His Word every day, and you should also be in the Word daily. Then prayer is so important. The Word says in James 4:2b-3 (NLT), "Yet you don't have what you want because you don't ask God for it. And even when you ask, you don't get it because your motives are all wrong—you want only what will give you pleasure." James is questioning our motivations here in this passage. Although we think our motivations are pure, this isn't always the case. When we come to God, asking for an outcome out of negative motivations will result in an outcome that we don't expect from Him. God already knows our motives and our hearts are deceptively wicked. So if we ask God for something for the wrong reasons, we'll never get what we truly want.

So check your heart before you check in with the Lord. Is your heart in alignment with His Word and with His character? Remember "so if you sinful people know how to give good gifts to your children, how much more will your heavenly Father give good gifts to those who ask him" (Matthew 7:11, NKJV). He is ready and prepared to give you what you want and need as long as your heart and your motives are right.

The baby who doesn't get to come home with you from the hospital is already in the arms of Jesus. Now, it's your turn to become a child of God, and when you are called home not only will you be with our Savior, but you have a great hope of seeing your loved one again. So, how does a person get there? You must be born again. "That if you confess with your mouth the Lord Jesus and believe in your heart that God has raised Him from the dead, you will be saved. For with the heart one believes unto righteousness, and with the mouth confession is made unto salvation" (Romans 10:9–10, NKJV). It's clear here in His Word. Listen, the Word always has the final say! We must repent of all our sins and then ask Jesus in our hearts. It's truly that simple.

Now, you might ask how this strength for the journey comes into play. In Nehemiah 8:10 (NKJV) it says, "The joy of the lord is your strength." So what is the joy of the Lord? It is an understanding of God's forgiveness. God's forgiveness doesn't come because you're sorry or because you have earned it. God's forgiveness is only and entirely the result of what Jesus Christ did for us on the cross. Conviction is meant to bring us to the end of ourselves, to bring us back to the cross, and that gives us joy. The person with joy doesn't dwell on the trials of life, though they know they are there, but the trials bring us to an intimate knowledge of who God is. To know

> *that Christ may dwell in your hearts through faith; that you, being rooted and grounded in love, may be able to comprehend with all the saints what is the width and length and depth and height—to know the love of Christ which passes knowledge; that you may be filled with all the fullness of God.*

Ephesians 3:17–19 (NKJV)

This is true joy, not happiness because happiness depends on emotion, but joy comes from the Lord. It is knowing that in the face of great adversity you are still loved and your faith in God will sustain you. Do you have the joy of the Lord, and is He your strength?

> *Jesus, with all the chaos going on all around me, I am asking for Your joy, Your peace, and Your strength that only You can give me. In Jesus' name. Amen.*

DAY 45:

"Come as You Are"

"Come and let us return [in repentance] to the Lord, For He has torn us, but He will heal us; He has wounded us, but He will bandage us."

Hosea 6:1AMP)

I just love autumn. It shows us how beautiful it is to let things go. Autumn is a season of beautiful fall colors that precede the winter season. It's a time of letting go of past things. I once heard that we need to let go of stuff, such as…letting go of caring what others think about you, letting go of unrealistic goals. Just let go of anything that does not glorify Jesus. Holding onto past wounds and the pain of the past and even the pain of the present will lead you to a life of devastation and loss. My husband has this saying, "It's none of my business what other people think about me." He's so right, and I absolutely love this saying.

I think letting go means forgiveness. We need to learn to forgive others, and it says in Ephesians 4:32 (NKJV), "And be kind to one another, tenderhearted, forgiving one another, even as God in Christ forgave you." Forgiveness is not for the other person who may have hurt you but for you to be set free of their crime toward you. It was once explained to me, and it was very powerful…it's like drinking poison and expecting it to harm the other person. The poison will kill you, not the other person who has wounded you. Like drinking poison, holding onto unforgiveness actually hurts you and not the other person.

So I'll leave it right here with you. "Judge not, and you shall not be judged. Condemn not, and you shall not be condemned. Forgive, and you will be forgiven" (Luke 6:37, NKJV). You have been forgiven much by the Father in heaven; even Jesus modeled forgiveness while on the cross. If Jesus can forgive those who killed Him, can you forgive those who have committed much lesser crimes against you? By holding onto unforgiveness for someone, you are telling God that your ways are better than His. That, my friends, is blasphemous.

There is a very powerful scene from the movie *The Shack* where the lead character, "Mac," is taken into this cave behind a waterfall. In this cave, the character representing a messenger of God talks to Mac about forgiveness and judgment. Mac blamed God for taking his youngest daughter, who died at the hands of a serial killer/rapist. The messenger talks to Mac about how he feels about the person who committed this heinous act against his little girl. She then asks Mac if he blamed God. Then she went on to tell Mac that God is asking Him to choose between his two remaining children…one will spend eternity in heaven, and the other will be condemned to hell. Mac insists that he won't make that decision; he can't make that decision. He then tells the messenger, "Take me instead." This is how God views all His children. He wants none of His children to be condemned to hell, but it's a decision we make on our own. Holding onto unforgiveness is a surefire ticket to hell.

Can you forgive someone who has harmed you in some irreparable way? Maybe that someone is you. Maybe you're blaming yourself for the pain that you are experiencing. You are living in a self-made prison. No matter who is to blame, you must let go of the pain and forgive. It's not optional…just let it all go!

Let go of the pain…let go of the hurt…let go of the betrayal…let go of the anger. My prayer for you today is that you just let it go and watch God move in your life in a mighty way. Letting go will set you free, so just let it go! Now is such a good time to start and just let it go. What would you like to let go in your life?

Jesus, help me forgive anyone who I believe has harmed me. I don't want to carry this pain anymore. I want to give it all to You. Help me forgive myself for anything I believe is my fault. I can't take it anymore, so I leave it at Your feet. Help others to forgive me if I have wronged them in any way. Lord, that was not my intention. In Jesus' name. Amen.

DAY 46:

"Stand Up and Walk"

Just then some people brought a paraplegic man to him, lying on a sleeping mat. When Jesus perceived the strong faith within their hearts, he said to the paralyzed man, "My son, be encouraged, for your sins have been forgiven." These words prompted some of the religious scholars to think, "Why, that's nothing but blasphemy!" Jesus supernaturally perceived their thoughts, and said to them, "Why do you carry such evil in your hearts? Which is easier to say, 'Your sins are forgiven,' or, 'Stand up and walk!'? But now, to convince you that the Son of Man has been given authority to forgive sins, I say to this man, 'Stand up, pick up your mat, and walk home.'" Immediately the man sprang to his feet and left for home. When the crowds witnessed this miracle, they were awestruck. They shouted praises to God because he had given such authority to human beings.

Matthew 9:2–8 (TPT)

What is a miracle? There are everyday, little miracles such as the next breath you breathe or the next beat of your heart. These miracles don't even get noticed. Then there are miracles that are more supernatural in nature. These miracles include supernatural healing, financial miracles that come out of nowhere at just the time needed, or how about the prodigal son coming home? Now this is not an exhaustive list by any means. "Miracle" is a word that is thrown around without much thought, but rarely when we say the word do we expect a divine intervention by God Himself.

Have you ever seen a miracle? I have seen many…my children are my biggest miracles, all four of them. The day they were born was the most amazing day of my life. Those tiny little humans that Jesus gave to me. The miracle of birth truly is a miracle. The miracle of life is beautiful, but what happens when you don't bring that baby home? Is it still a miracle? Many would say, "Where was the miracle in this?" I would tell you any life is a miracle.

My first son went to heaven shortly after birth. I couldn't understand at that time why this was happening to me, but now I truly get it. I was picked by God Himself for this assignment…this is where this ministry was birthed out of my deepest pain. Through my son's very brief life, I was forced to face some inner wounds that may have never been healed without God's intervention…His intervention just so happened to occur at the death of my little boy. This wasn't a sudden revelation by any means. This was something that developed over many years. But if I had not given birth to my son and watched him pass away, I'm not sure I would have obtained the healing I so desperately needed in other parts of my life.

God has a way of taking something that was meant for evil…meant to destroy us, but He uses the circumstances and reorders our life if we cooperate with the process. The death of a child is devastating! I'm not sure you ever really get over it. But I do believe you obtain strength from it. You are more able to endure other storms in your life. Life just has a way of keeping us in a cycle of storms. You're either currently in a storm, coming out of a storm, or preparing to enter a storm. Those are the facts. If we look hard enough, we will find the miracle in the storm. Yes, you may need to get on the other side of the storm before you realize there was a miracle in it, but I believe you will look back one day and say there was a miracle that resulted from your storm…I know I did.

Miracles do happen every day, but sometimes they are harder to find, especially when you're looking for a miracle in the storm. But God is faithful, and He will step into your life and your situation. You will have to seek Him out of a hunger for Him, but you will find Him when you seek Him with your whole heart. How many times have we sought to blame God for the bad things in our life? But we seldom give Him credit for the blessings in our life. Look for Him in *all* things; He is there. Miracles come out of our expectation…when you are expecting Him to come through, He will. What's the miracle you are expecting of God?

Jesus, as I look into Your eyes, help me see the miracles all around me, even the small ones.
Draw me closer to Your heart and come into any area that needs healing. In Jesus' name.
Amen.

DAY 47:

"Be Healed"

"God spoke the words 'Be healed,' and we were healed, delivered from death's door! So lift your hands and give thanks to God for his marvelous kindness and for his miracles of mercy for those he loves!

Psalm 107:20 (TPT)

I was very fortunate and blessed to have great in-laws. My husband's parents were wonderful, godly people. Unfortunately, I was only able to know them for about three or four years before his mother passed away. Then my father-in-law passed away a little over a year later. This was truly an amazing couple.

I specifically remember a trip we took to Colorado with my husband's parents about a year into our marriage. My husband had gifted me a trip to a "captivating" retreat for women through Wild at Heart Ministries. I was excited to go to this retreat because my husband had raved about going to the men's version of this retreat called a Wild at Heart Bootcamp. But I was a little apprehensive to go alone. So my husband and his parents went and stayed in a condo not far away from the place where I would be staying. The drive through the mountains was stunning to say the least. I remember like yesterday as we drove along the tight mountain highway, seeing snow in the trees and the sunshine bearing down casting a beauty among the fresh virgin snow. As we drove, my husband's mother raised her little hand and simply said, "Oh Jesus, Jesus." Suddenly the whole car was filled with the Holy Spirit as if Jesus said, "You called…here I am." This was the point in time when I became aware of what a godly woman my mother-in-law was and how blessed I was to be part of her family. In my lifetime, I have never known anyone more selfless and loving than this couple.

They had been married just over sixty years when she passed away. This was a brutal time for the family, as her husband and their sons were completely numb, as she was the glue that held their family together. My father-in-law was a terrific man, a veteran of the US Air Force for thirty years and truly knew no strangers. He loved everyone he met and treated people with the utmost respect. I watched him as he would order food at a restaurant that he didn't really like, all because he knew his wife could eat it and really liked it. She loved to try different things, but unfortunately her body would not allow her to eat many things due to the impact of chemotherapy and radiation treatments for breast cancer that she had overcome some years before I met them. So he would order things he didn't really want because he knew she would be able to eat what he ordered. When the food arrived and she couldn't eat what she ordered, he gently offered his meal to her, and he ate what she couldn't even though he didn't really like it. Another example of his selflessness was when he would go to bed a few minutes ahead of her and lie down on her side of the bed so that she would have a warm bed to lie down on.

I have never known a couple to love each other the way my in-laws did. It was truly a match made in heaven. Unfortunately, when my mother-in-law passed away, her husband was completely lost and alone. He couldn't go back to his own home because everywhere he looked, he saw reminders of his lost love. She had been gone for about a year when my father-in-law came to visit for a while. The conversation had turned to his wife, and sadness was all over his face. He didn't understand why God wouldn't take him home because he simply lost the desire to live without his wife. My husband asked his dad, "Dad, do you think the reason why you haven't gone home to heaven is because you idolized Mom?" A prompt "*no*" came from his mouth. He went to bed shortly after that conversation and awoke the next morning, came downstairs for breakfast, and said, "I think you're right; I did idolize your mom. I repented of that last night, and the good Lord forgave me." He left a few days later to spend some time with one of my husband's brothers in Michigan. He was to return to our house for Thanksgiving about a month later. My husband got a call from his brother the day before he was supposed to leave and told us he had passed away suddenly with no expectation.

We believe that my husband's dad made everything right with God and that he was now at peace with himself and God. God rewarded his obedience and brought him home. I remember him telling me after the first Christmas, about two and a half months after his sweetie passed away, "Jean, I don't think I can take another holiday without my sweetie." He loved his family more than life itself, but his bride meant the world to him, and he didn't want to experience anything without her. He died just before the next big holiday…Thanksgiving. God granted his request.

Not every marriage is like their marriage. Nowadays, I would say there's a special kind of love that only comes along for the lucky few. The truly blessed ones. They had their fair share of adversity, but they never let anything or anyone come between them. They worked out their differences whenever they arose, and they ended every argument with "I love you." Love is what held this family together, and love led them home to Jesus. Jesus was at the center of their marriage…as every marriage should be.

First Corinthians 13:13 (NLT) says, "Three things will last forever—faith, hope, and love—and the greatest of these is love." This verse was readily apparent in the lives of my husband's parents. They let the glory of the Lord shine through them in everything they did. Their selflessness was a perfect example of the love of Jesus for all of us. I learned a lot in the short time I knew them, but I'm thankful to

God for every minute. Like my in-laws, do you have the kind of love that when people look at you, they say, "I see Jesus in them"?

Jesus, I pray when people see me that they see You. *Help me get to the end of me so people can see* You *in me. Use me and mold me into what You want me to be. In Jesus' name. Amen.*

DAY 48:

"Return"

"Return and tell Hezekiah the leader of My people, 'Thus says the Lord, the God of David your father: "I have heard your prayer, I have seen your tears; surely I will heal you. On the third day you shall go up to the house of the Lord."'"

2 Kings 20:5 (NKJV)

Today we decided to do something a little different. The following is the story of one of our volunteers at Angels in Waiting 91:4. As you will soon learn, she is well acquainted with loss and grief. Listen to this powerful story of overcoming adversity.

"When you're young, you think life will be like a fairytale. You marry the man of your dreams, have babies, and live life happily ever after. Isn't that what the movies tell us? But, in reality, life isn't a fairy tale. You never know what a day will bring. We do everything within our power to make our dreams come true. But God has His own plans for our life, and His ways are higher than our ways. Rarely do our plans match what He has in store for us. If only we would follow His plan for our life.

"I married a wonderful young man when I was nineteen years old, but he wasn't a Christian when we married. But fortunately, God's plan and my plan seemed to merge together, and my husband got saved, and we had a little girl together. This was when things turned bad. My husband was diagnosed with a brain tumor at the age of thirty-three. I lost him within one year of the diagnosis. I was shattered, and my fairytale quickly turned into a nightmare.

"Years later, I married again and was married for over thirty years when my second husband was diagnosed with lung cancer, and it had spread to his brain. I was in my sixties at the time of the diagnosis, and I lost my second husband in less than a year. I was devastated to be a widow yet again.

"All I can say is life is not a fairy tale! Life has many twists and turns that we never expect. But we live in a fallen world under the authority of a wicked ruler. He will learn about the plans God has for us and seek to destroy those plans and our relationship with God. I didn't understand why my life had turned out the way it did, and I felt alone and, at times, very angry. Yet through it all, God was faithful! He stayed with me and helped me through the lonely days and nights; He never left my side through all the heartache and pain I had experienced.

"I wish I could say that through all this I never questioned God, but I truthfully didn't understand any of it. It took a long time for the sharpness of my losses to become dull and not cut me to the quick. Yet I can say today that my God knows exactly what He's doing; He truly does lead us through the valley of the shadow of death. He does lead me beside the quiet waters and helps me to find peace in all situations. Look, if I'm being honest with you, I still don't understand it all, but I do know that God does have a plan for my life. Fortunately, I know one day I will be greeted by both of my wonderful husbands at the gate of heaven."

I know when we first marry the love of our life, we never expect for it to end in death. But a true love story always ends in pain for one person or the other. Most of us don't have to go through life having lost two spouses like our volunteer. And rarely do people hold onto their faith and hope when life hands us these kinds of twists and turns. But when we are able to turn our eyes to Jesus, He really will take our test and turn it into a testimony. Think of the people you may know who have been through trials like this precious lady. Did you learn anything about life through the way they handled adversity? I know I have had these kinds of people, like our volunteer, who inspire me to do better. When we come to the end of ourselves and live the life He has planned for us, no matter the cost, then we, too, can be an inspiration for someone else who has not yet trodden the path. There is a quote from an unknown person that I just love that speaks to this very well…"God is still God, God is still good to God be the glory"! Through all the trials you may be going through, can you say to God be the glory?

Jesus, I ask You to help me come to the end of myself and find the person You created me to be. Heal me in all areas of the grief I am trying to carry on my own. I admit I need You, Lord.

In Jesus' name. Amen.

DAY 49:

"Save Me"

"Heal me, O Lord, and I will be healed; Save me and I will be saved, For You are my praise."

Jeremiah 17:14 (AMP)

Postpartum depression is a very difficult area of our lives to try to understand. You carry this precious baby for nine months, and then your bundle of joy comes, and you feel much less than joyful. I struggled very hard with one of my own pregnancies. Having this beautiful baby and all these emotions running through you. Wondering what's wrong with you? *Why can't I be happy? What is my issue?*

Let me make something very clear—it has nothing to do with your baby! It is an imbalance in your hormones. This is much more common than you'd think. In fact, there are approximately 3 million cases diagnosed in the US every year, according to the Mayo Clinic. Some famous people have experienced this in their own lives: Brooke Shields, Drew Barrymore, Princess Diana, Sarah Michelle Gellar, and many others. Postpartum depression affects everyone from every socioeconomic class. It is an equal opportunity offender. Yet there is some kind of stigma attached to this that causes women not to want to admit it has happened to them because of the fear of being looked at as if they're crazy. It is a very common condition, yet it is also very isolating. You want to pull away from everyone, including your own baby. But remember you are not alone.

We know it's a hormone imbalance…it's different from the baby blues; the baby blues go away shortly after birth. It's not that the mother doesn't want the child or wants to harm the child. It makes Mommy feel as though she's completely nuts. It causes you not to bond with your child. You may only have it once and never have it again. Or you could experience it with every pregnancy. Because the bonding doesn't immediately occur doesn't mean you can't bond with that child later. It may be more difficult for you to bond with this child later because they didn't get the maternal bond they needed at an early age from mommy. More often than not, someone else is stepping in for mom and filling her shoes to give the baby what is needed. Children who have a mommy who has experienced postpartum depression will grow up just fine; this is yet another thing that a mom experiencing this debilitating problem worries about. This is where a mother will carry this guilt for her whole life if it isn't dealt with properly. You must guard your mind and your heart.

It is important to understand that this is a ploy of the enemy…remember he seeks to steal, kill, and destroy. So it is easy to understand that the enemy would seek to separate a child from its mother even at birth. At the time of birth, there is no one more important to a baby than Mommy. So who would the devil come after? Mommy. Communication with caregivers and loved ones is vital. Seek wise counsel and be honest with them about everything you are feeling. Communicate with your loved ones and your counselors (pastoral, mentors, and clinical), and let them know exactly how you are feeling. Above all seek the Lord; remember He says in Matthew 11:28–30 (NLT):

> *Then Jesus said, "Come to me, all of you who are weary and carry heavy burdens, and I will give you rest. Take my yoke upon you. Let me teach you, because I am humble and gentle at heart, and you will find rest for your souls. For my yoke is easy to bear, and the burden I give you is light."*

Jesus is asking you to give up all the cares and worries that weigh you down. He is telling you to allow Him to bear your burdens. Healing is always found in Jesus! Psalm 147:3 (NKJV) says, "He heals the brokenhearted And binds up their wounds." Jesus is good in all His ways, and His way is not burdensome or difficult. Jesus' great desire is that we find the rest we so desperately need, which is a rest that only He can give. Have you given Jesus all your hurts, burdens, and pain?

Jesus, I am giving You all my hurts and burdens. Help me to forgive myself when I feel less than what You created me to be. In Jesus' name. Amen.

DAY 50:

"The Kiss of Peace"

"This is the one who gives his strength and might to his people.
This is the Lord giving us his kiss of peace."

Psalm 29:11 (TPT)

I can just see the scene in the upper room before Jesus was crucified. This should have been a celebration of the Passover feast. The Passover celebration was an ordinance set by God Himself to remember the exodus of the nation of Israel from Egyptian captivity. This was a feast established to remember the final plague against Egypt and Pharaoh. The story is told in the book of Exodus:

> *For I will pass through the land of Egypt on that night and will strike all the firstborn in the land of Egypt, both man and beast; and against all the gods of Egypt I will execute judgment: I am the Lord. Now the blood shall be a sign for you on the houses where you are. And when I see the blood, I will pass over you; and the plague shall not be on you to destroy you when I strike the land of Egypt.*

Exodus 12:12–13 (NKJV)

The Jews were the only people in Egypt to know about the slaughter that was about to occur; therefore, the Israelites were spared the death of the firstborn. The feast commemorates that night and was to be celebrated every year by the people of Israel.

Jesus and His disciples were gathered in the upper room to celebrate the Passover. But this was no ordinary Passover celebration. On this night in the upper room, Jesus would prophesy His crucifixion and let the twelve disciples know that one of them would betray Him. We all now know that Judas was the one who betrayed Him. All of the disciples asked Jesus if it was them who would betray Him. Jesus simply said it is the one who dips His bread in the cup with me. Can you just imagine watching Judas drink from the cup and Him knowing he was the one who would betray Him? This meal is now known as communion. Jesus declares that it would have been better if His betrayer had not been born. Then Judas had the gall to ask Jesus, "Rabbi, is it I?" All Jesus said to him was, "You have said it." After the communion meal, Jesus departed to Gethsemane to pray. Upon His return, Jesus was met by Judas and a multitude of soldiers. Judas came up to Jesus and kissed Him on the cheek. "But Jesus said to him, 'Judas, are you betraying the Son of Man with a kiss?'" (Luke 22:48, NKJV).

Betrayal is similar to an act of treason. It is the ultimate act of disloyalty. It is the death of a relationship between the betrayer and the victim of betrayal. The act of betrayal leaves in its wake a massive amount of pain and heartache. Without Jesus, this pain, heartache, and lack of trusting people can last decades or more. Even with inviting Jesus into the wound, the lack of trust can be a huge issue for the victim. Trust takes time and many, many acts to build it. Yet trust can also be torn down in an instant with one single act of betrayal. Once a person is betrayed, it becomes very difficult to trust anyone. You constantly are questioning the motives of those around you, and your eyes are always scanning the horizon looking for reasons to not allow someone to get close to you. But you cannot allow your relationship with one person to determine your relationship with everyone else in your circle. Allow yourself to hope, believe, and trust again. Refuse to let one person who hurt you define how you respond to everyone else.

Once trust is broken, it is easier to put up a wall around your heart than to risk it being broken again. But these trust issues can destroy current and future relationships with others. We need each other and we are not meant to do life alone. God created us to be in relationship. When we isolate ourselves from the world, we become easy prey for the enemy to attack. We must learn to trust again…start with God. After all He has never left you nor forsaken you. "You will keep in perfect peace all who trust in you, all whose thoughts are fixed on you! Trust in the Lord always, for the Lord God is the eternal Rock" (Isaiah 26:3–4, NLT). Allow Him to guide you in everything you do and with every relationship that you have. Ask Him for His wisdom and discernment, and He will give you strength to move forward one step at a time. Betrayal hurts, but it doesn't have to paralyze you in the other areas of your life. Trusting is a vital part of life. Marriages cannot survive without trust or even relationship with family or loved one. Not even can business relationships survive without trust. Remember what the Lord tells us in Jeremiah 29:11 (NKJV), "For I know the thoughts that I think toward you, says the Lord, thoughts of peace and not of evil, to give you a future and a hope." Jesus will never lead you wrong; in Him we can trust with our lives. Surender to Him all your hopes, dreams, and trust issues. He will never let you down! Do you struggle with trust issues from a betrayal?

Jesus, my heart has broken into a million pieces by betrayal. I need You to come into this place and heal my heart. I know it is a place that only You can heal. In Jesus' name. Amen.

DAY 51:

"Sweetness to Our Soul"

"Nothing is more appealing than speaking beautiful, life-giving words. For they release sweetness to our souls and inner healing to our spirits."

Proverbs 16:24 (TPT)

Are you a glass-half-full or a glass-half-empty kind of person? How you answer that question is likely how you speak about your life. What you speak is so important. The Bible says in Proverbs 18:21 (NKJV) that "death and life are in the power of the tongue, and those who love it will eat its fruit." Clearly speaking the right words over your life is vitally important in your life. Many times, it will determine the circumstances of your life. I'm sure you have heard the term "self-fulfilling prophecy"… basically, this means whatever you speak will come to pass.

Personally, I'm learning what I speak will come to pass! And what we allow others to speak over us can also come to pass. Think about all the ways someone can speak a negative outcome over your life. You can receive a negative doctor's report that condemns you to death or a shortened life. You can have people speak all kinds of negative words over your life. How you receive or don't receive these words can determine whether or not these words come to pass.

So why not speak life over a negative situation? You may have a doctor tell you that you are not capable of having a baby. Speak life over that word, "I am equipped to have a child, and God will make a way where there seems to be no way." You may have just lost a baby…someone says, "Well, it just wasn't meant to be for you." Don't receive that word and speak life, "I will have a baby of my own." The Bible tells us to claim our authority that has been earned for us by Jesus on the cross at Calvary. Speak to the mountains that are in your way (Mark 11:23).

I'm not sure what mountain you have in your life, but I can assure you that if you have the faith of a mustard seed to decree and declare to that mountain, it will fall into the sea. Your situation is not hopeless! We have a miracle-working God. Jesus died on a cross for you and for me to ransom us from the evil one. He cares for us, and He wants to give us good gifts! (See James 1:17.)

I am reminded of a piece of scripture in the book of Deuteronomy in chapter 6:1–3 (NIV). This scripture says:

These are the commands, decrees and laws the Lord your God directed me to teach you to observe in the land that you are crossing the Jordan to possess, so that you, your children and their children after them may fear the Lord your God as long as you live by keeping all his decrees and commands that I give you, and so that you may enjoy long life. Hear, Israel, and be careful to obey so that it may go well with you and that you may increase greatly in a land flowing with milk and honey, just as the Lord, the God of your ancestors, promised you.

Did you catch the word "decrees" there? God is telling His people to decree the Word of God over their life, to keep His commandments and walk in them by being careful to obey them. By obeying the Word, He guaranteed a prosperous and joyful life.

What and how you speak matters. Speak life instead of death. Speak prosperity instead of poverty. Speak faith over fear. Be determined that no matter what the natural world tells you, you will speak what the Word of God says over your particular situation. Find the specific scriptures and decree and declare the promises of God over your mountain. Choose this day how you want to live and speak it out. The devil hates when we speak out the Word of God, so why not declare it today loudly?

Lord, help me speak only Your truths. I need to know You and hear You so I can drown out all the other voices and lean into You. In Jesus' name. Amen.

DAY 52:

"Grace upon Grace"

"And God, the source of shalom, will soon crush the Adversary under your feet. The grace of our Lord Yeshua be with you."

Romans 16:20 (CJB)

The title of this is so important because the Lord even began giving me the little details about how to function. We found a perfect box at a local retailer that had Psalm 91:4 on the box. We began buying these boxes until we could no longer get them. Then we designed one with our own logo. In these delivery boxes, we place twenty-five gowns. Why twenty-five gowns? Why not ten or even fifty? The simple answer is that the Lord told me to put twenty-five gowns in the boxes. The biblical meaning of the number twenty-five is "grace upon grace." God spoke to me and told me that He was placing grace upon grace to the families that receive these gowns. My son came and told me, "Do you know what twenty-five means biblically?" He then told me it means grace upon grace. God will use those who don't know Him yet to deliver His messages of confirmation.

God shows us both mercy and grace, but they are not the same. Mercy withholds a punishment that we deserve. Grace gives us blessings that we don't deserve. God is merciful in not extending to us the punishment that our sin deserves. Through His offering His one and only Son, Jesus Christ, He extends grace to us. Without His grace, we are enemies of God, and we are deserving of the punishment of eternal death because of our sin. But through Jesus, we are granted eternal life with Him in heaven.

God has done something that few of us, if any, can do on our own. We rarely extend mercy to our enemies, let alone grace. But God gives us both mercy and grace.

So you might be asking yourself, *What then is grace upon grace?* If grace is the unmerited favor and blessing of God, what does it mean to have grace upon grace? I like how the Amplified Bible describes grace upon grace as written in John 1:16: "For out of His fullness [the superabundance of His grace and truth] we have all received grace upon grace [spiritual blessing upon spiritual blessing, favor upon favor, and gift heaped upon gift]." It doesn't really get any clearer than that. Wouldn't you like to receive a superabundance of His grace? Honestly, I have a hard time comprehending that kind of grace. But that is exactly what God offers us.

Jesus fulfills grace upon grace. From His fullness we receive an abundance of His grace. He gives us favor and more favor, blessing and more blessing; that is a glimpse of grace upon grace. When we surrender to Him and His ways, that superabundance of His grace is available to us every single day.

Our babies who have gone on ahead of us are already bathing in this superabundant grace. One day, when our time on this earth is through, we, as followers of Jesus Christ, will also live in that magnificent grace. But the beauty of God is that it is also available to us before we get to heaven; John 10:10 says that even though the enemy seeks to destroy us, Jesus has given us abundant life…right here, right now.

We don't often understand John 10:10 because of the storms that we endure. But if we seek Him first and His righteousness, as Jesus describes in Matthew 6, He makes it clear that all things will be given to us also. Jesus cares about us and wants us to experience His goodness in every area of our life. But we can't experience His fullness if we are stuck wallowing in self-pity or sorrow. That is not God's will for us. Mourning is but for a season…then we are to live our best life according to His Word and be a testimony for someone else. Remember the gospel comes to us on its way to someone else. So let your test become your testimony. Your story may help free someone else from a lifetime of bondage. Are you ready to receive your healing and tell your story?

Jesus, thank You for Your mercy and Your grace. I am eternally grateful. Teach me to give grace upon grace to others as You place them in my life. In Jesus' name. Amen.

DAY 53:

"This Is Not Our Home"

Now He who has prepared us for this very thing is God, who also has given us the Spirit as a guarantee. So we are always confident, knowing that while we are at home in the body we are absent from the Lord. For we walk by faith, not by sight. We are confident, yes, well pleased rather to be absent from the body and to be present with the Lord.

2 Corinthians 5:5–8 (NKJV)

As a Christian, we often refer to our body as the temple of the Lord. We are a dwelling place for the Holy Spirit. In today's scripture reference, it talks about how this body we live in now, and the earth we live on, is a temporary home at best. In 2 Corinthians 5, verse 2, it says that we groan, earnestly desiring to be clothed with our habitation. That is not referring to the body we currently live in but is referring to our heavenly home. This is a place not made by human hands but a mansion built and designed especially for us by God Himself. Can you imagine that?

Think of this—your loved one who passed before you, more than likely, there was something wrong that your baby didn't quite form right or had a serious health issue that resulted in their death. Now imagine your baby taking its first breath in heaven, breathing in the purest of air. Taking in the light that is the glory of the Lord for the very first time. Their little body has no birth defect, no health issue, and no struggle to live in the earthly tent they were born with. Now they are living in a perfect body with no blemish, no fault, not even a wrinkle. I have heard some who have been transported to heaven say that your child is there waiting for you to arrive. You will be given a choice to raise your child from the age of their death, or you can choose to walk with them from the age that they would be now. I can't back that up with Scripture, but that is so like our God to give us the opportunity to raise a child that we may have lost decades ago, or maybe your loss occurred just yesterday. It is the Father's nature to give us such a wonderful gift…He really is a good, good Father.

Our children get to frolic with the Father, with Jesus, and with the Holy Spirit in the most perfect place imaginable. It's not some wispy, cloudy kind of place where we sit on a cloud playing a harp singing to the Father for all eternity. It is a place with streets of gold, with gates made from a single pearl, and with a temple whose foundation is made from the most precious of stones. The Word of God says He designed all of that for us, and then He creates a mansion that is specific to you. We can only imagine a glimpse of the magnificence of heaven, not to mention the vastness of it all. The Bible says that the

Father's robe, when He enters into the room, fills the temple. Clearly, He likes nice things that are lavish beyond compare.

The Father does not have a poverty spirit, and He doesn't expect us to have one either. He seeks to bless us beyond our wildest imaginations. He only wants the best for us. Our eternal life in heaven will be way beyond comparison. Nothing on this earth can hold a candle to the least in heaven. Our babies who have gone on ahead of us never experienced the travails of this world. Instead, they went from this old, broken-down tent straight to a palace in the sky. Though we mourn for them, and rightly so, they didn't spend one second in this world of evil. Selfishly we wish we had them here with us to hug and to hold, to cuddle, and to raise. But they are waiting for you now in the most glorious place. This brings to mind James 4:14 (TPT), which says, "But you don't have a clue what tomorrow may bring. For your fleeting life is but a warm breath of air that is visible in the cold only for a moment and then vanishes!"

Allow yourself to be taken away, if even for only a moment, by your imagination into the heavenly realm. Now imagine seeing your perfect child face to face for the very first time. Looking into their perfect eyes and speaking with them like no time has ever passed you by. My friends, I long for that day, and I imagine you do too. What is the first thing you want to see when you get to heaven?

Sweet Heavenly Father, I long for the day I get to see You face to face. My home is not here, for I am only passing by. Heal my heart and help me wait patiently for You. Hide me away in Your secret place. I love You, Lord. Amen.

DAY 54:

"Clarity in the Storm"

"For God is not the author of confusion but of peace, as in all the churches of the saints."

1 Corinthians 14:33(NKJV)

There are times in our life when it feels as though we are living in a storm where we experience much pain and loss in our lives. Sometimes these storms turn into seasons of heartache. How you handle these seasons can determine your outlook on the rest of your life. Do you look for the positive in everything? The "every cloud has a silver lining" mentality. Or do you view life as nothing good could ever come of the trials you've been through? These are two drastically different approaches to handling the day-to-day cycles of life.

Some people experience more storms than others. Why this happens is a question that only God can answer. We have a friend who is also a volunteer in our ministry who has endured more trials than most other people. I can't tell her whole story here in this devotional, but I can give you a taste of the things she has had to endure.

On the morning of July 5th, 2020, her husband received an early morning phone call that their thirty-three-year-old son had passed away. He had so much life ahead of him, but unfortunately his life was cut short. He had a little girl, and her mother had passed away several months before. As you can imagine, there was much sadness and weeping over their son's death. That is the phone call no parent ever wants to receive. Due to COVID-19 restrictions, there was not much information like how he died, funeral restrictions, etc. She wasn't even able to see her son much in the time leading up to his death.

However, by God's grace, she had a chance meeting with him outside a gas station the Saturday before Mother's Day in May of 2020. Little did she know at that time that this would be the last time she would see her son. Through her son's death, she ended up getting custody of her granddaughter, whom she is now raising. She would also later find out that the cause of death was an accidental overdose of his medications and also having fentanyl in his system. None of this was very encouraging and could have easily led her to a point of depression.

But she was able to hold onto her faith in Jesus, and she thanked Him for a not-so-coincidental meeting with her son at a gas station. She was grateful that God, knowing all things, would give her a chance to tell her son she loved him before he died. God was in the details, as always, knitting everything together, bringing good out of a tragedy. Her son was a US Army veteran and was honored in death with a flag that was given to his daughter, which I am sure will be a cherished reminder of her daddy.

No matter what storms may come, the key is to continue to love and trust God. Spend time in prayer and continuously stay in the His Word. This will keep you equipped to manage crises and stand strong and firm in any season. Choose to love, believe, and trust God with everything and every circumstance. One day the Lord will wipe away every tear from our eyes, and there will be no more death or sorrow or crying. There will be no more deep pain, for the former things will have passed away forever. Jesus promises us in His Word to make all things new.

Can you just imagine no more tears of sorrow or crying? No more death and no more heartache. No weeping or mourning of their loved ones who have passed away or died unexpectedly. No more pain of deep wounds or grief that will no longer exist! For the former things have passed away.

This mighty woman of God, through all of this and more deeply troubling circumstances, has continued to put her faith in the Lord. She is content in knowing that God makes all things new and will work out all her troubles and trials for her good and His glory. He truly does provide clarity in the storms. His peace becomes our peace when we put all our faith and trust in Him. No matter what life throws at us, the Lord is our strength. I love how the Passion Translation puts it in Psalm 28:7–8:

> *Yahweh is my strength and my wraparound shield. When I fully trust in you, help is on the way. I jump for joy and burst forth with ecstatic, passionate praise! I will sing songs of what you mean to me! You will be the inner strength of all your people, Yahweh, the mighty protector of all, and the saving strength for all your anointed ones.*

The Lord is your strength…knowing that, will you jump for joy no matter your circumstances?

> *Jesus, no matter the circumstances of what life brings me, help me feel Your love wrapped around me. I know in Your love I am safe. Come, Jesus, and show me Your love. In Jesus' mighty name. Amen.*

DAY 55:

"Perfect Peace"

"You keep in perfect peace one whose mind is stayed on You, because he trusts in You. Trust in Adonai forever, for the Lord Adonai is a Rock of ages."

Isaiah 26:3–4 (TLV)

As we sit in the middle of chaos all around us, I have peace in my heart, mind, and soul. This peace can only come from my precious Jesus. I am reminded in Galatians 5:22–23 (NKJV): "But the fruit of the Spirit is love, joy, *peace*, longsuffering, kindness, goodness, faithfulness, gentleness, self-control." This is an area we all need some work in. What if we lived in a world of kindness? Can you imagine how peace could come upon you, then? I love this verse in Psalm 85:10 (NKJV): "Mercy and truth have met together; Righteousness and *peace* have kissed." What does righteousness look like? Righteousness and peace have kissed like lovers who have been apart for such a long time. Think about that—it's just so beautiful! We must have this to get peace in our lives. My dear friends, we must get to the end of ourselves and trust Him for all things. We are so full of ourselves, and we can't even see it, but I assure you God can see it! It's time to find peace, and the only way to find it is to let go of ourselves. Be honest with God and seek Him today, and He will give you that sweet peace that only He can give you! Read Psalm 23; it is a beautiful picture of peace! Then just bask in His peace that only He can give you.

So what is perfect peace? I think that's a little subjective and could look and mean something different for each of us. Perfect peace means no inner turmoil to me. It's a state of being where there is no frantic frenzy of activity. A state where there is no anxiety or worry. A place where there is no need for competition or control. When I think of peace, I think of Jesus asleep in the bottom of the boat while there is a raging storm going on where the disciples are literally freaking out thinking they are about to die. Even when they wake Jesus up from His slumber, He looks around, sees the storm all around them, and simply says, "Peace be still." You can read the whole story in the book of Mark 4:35–41. I love this story for so many reasons, but the biggest reason is Jesus' casual attitude to a dire situation. The disciples were certain they were going to perish in the storm and that Jesus didn't care at all. Then toward the end of the story, Jesus asks His disciples, "Why are you so fearful? How is it that you have no faith?" (Mark 4:40, NKJV).

Put yourself in the disciples' sandals. How would you have answered Jesus? Would you have tried to justify your behavior? I mean, there was a legit storm that nearly capsized the boat. Do you think that would have been enough to satisfy the Lord? Or maybe you would have stood there in stone-cold silence wondering what had just happened. What Jesus did by rebuking the waves was nothing short of a miracle. Maybe you would have reacted like the disciples and said, "Wow, even the wind and the waves obey Him."

Now think about your storm. It isn't a physical weather phenomenon, but it's a storm nonetheless. Your storm undoubtedly comes with a lot of stress, a lot of worry, and a lot of unanswered questions. But have you lost your faith in the middle of the storm? Are you afraid and don't know which way to turn? This is exactly where the disciples were in the middle of a tempest that threatened their lives. They didn't have any of the answers, and they had no clue what to do next. When all the while they had every answer to every question they ever had asleep in the bottom of their boat. The disciples had been around Jesus enough to know that He didn't get flustered by anything, and He knew the right way to turn every time. He never made a mistake, and He never sinned. Jesus is perfect in every possible way.

So is Jesus asleep in your boat while you are worried, concerned, and flustered by what is happening all around you? I believe He would tell you the same thing He told the disciples, "Where is your faith?" Do you believe that Jesus can handle your problems? I can say assuredly that He can handle your mess…if you let Him. Maybe all it takes is you crying out to Him for help! Keep your mind on Him and keep trusting Him no matter what it looks like in the natural. What does peace look like to you?

Jesus, I am in a storm. I feel like it's spinning out of control. I am turning to You for perfect peace in this situation. Come, Lord Jesus, give me what only You can give me. In Jesus' name. Amen.

DAY 56:

"I Will Exalt You"

Lord, I will exalt you and lift you high, for you have lifted me up on high! Over all my boasting, gloating enemies, you made me to triumph. O Lord, my healing God, I cried out for a miracle, and you healed me! You brought me back from the brink of death, from the depths below. Now here I am, alive and well, fully restored!

Psalm 30:1-3 (TPT)

When something bad happens in our life, we seldom turn to praise and worship. There is nothing within us that says, "You know, things are pretty crummy right now. I should start praising God for all this." It seems so counterintuitive. The flesh fights the spirit in everything. But God is never logical, and very seldom do His ways make sense to us. But have you ever noticed that when you do something your spirit is telling you to do, even though it may not make any sense whatsoever, things tend to work out much better than you thought they would? The simple fact is His ways are better than our ways every single time. There has never been a time when His plans don't work out for us. It's only when we step out of alignment with His will for us that things turn south.

I love today's passage from Psalm 30. If you continue on just a little further in this Psalm, in the second half of verse 5 (NKJV), it says, "Weeping may endure for a night, but joy comes in the morning." There is a season of life when we will endure times of weeping; it's the cycle of life, but joy will come again. You will wake up one day and realize you're no longer on this steep climb but have arrived on a level plateau. It is a place of rest and peace. If you are diligent in seeking Him in these times of trial that are so exhausting, you will come to that place where you will be able to say, as King David said in Psalm 30:11 (NKJV), "You have turned for me my mourning into dancing; You have put off my sackcloth and clothed me with gladness."

It's not always easy to go from mourning to dancing. Let's face it—a lot of times we are just hoping to survive the day. Then we have the perspective where we work ourselves into a frenzy just trying to fill our lives with stuff and listening to TED Talks about how we can be the best me if we just perform steps one, two, three. Have you noticed the stuff never makes you happy long term? A new car loses its luster. A new house becomes new problems that have to be dealt with. A new relationship isn't what it once was in the beginning…the infatuation is gone. All the weight you lost comes back, and no matter how hard some of us try, we all get old. But Jesus promises us eternal life in heaven living in a place where there are no tears, no sadness, no bills, no worries, no stress. As a believer in Jesus Christ, this earth is not our home. We are only passing through on our way to eternal glory.

Here on earth, we are under a constant barrage of the devil's lies. If we are not careful, we come into agreement with those lies. We must repent and come out of agreement by speaking His Word over our situations. Never buy into the lies! The devil's promises are always false and will never get you where he says they will take you. The devil is a liar and the father of all lies (see John 8:44). However, when our thoughts are aligned with God's Word, the devil can't lie to us. That means not letting our thoughts run wild but checking our thoughts against the truth of God's Word. The apostle Paul urges us to think on whatever is true, noble, lovely, and praiseworthy. This is how we get our minds right and come into alignment with God's plan for our life.

It comes down to taking every thought captive and presenting it before the Lord. If the thoughts align with His will, then we can keep moving in that direction. If our thoughts are contrary to the Word of God, then we have to trash it and realize that it's probably the enemy seeking to get us to move off the path God has us on. With continual practice, it gets easier to spot the inconsistencies between what you're hearing and what God promises. You will get faster at taking thoughts captive, speaking against the lies, and realigning with truth. Ask for God to help you spot the lies and remind you of the truth so you can more easily fight back. When you begin to take back some territory, celebrate with God. He wants you to live a victorious life, and He wants you to win the battlefield of your mind. When you are able to put some wins together by turning your mourning into dancing, your praise will be more powerful than ever before. Your praise is a weapon. I love the story of King Jehoshaphat, King of Judah. Judah had come out to battle against overwhelming odds in fighting against Ammon, Moab, and Mount Seir in 2 Chronicles 20. "And Jehoshaphat feared, and set himself to seek the Lord, and proclaimed a fast throughout all Judah. So Judah gathered together to ask help from the Lord; and from all the cities of Judah they came to seek the Lord" (2 Chronicles 20:3–4, NKJV). God gave Jehoshaphat some unusual instructions. He told them to sing songs of praise. What? No battle strategy? No weapons of mass destruction? What possible good could singing praise and worship hymns do against a vast army set to destroy you? Well, let's see what happens:

> So they rose early in the morning and went out into the Wilderness of Tekoa; and as they went out, Jehoshaphat stood and said, "Hear me, O Judah and you inhabitants of Jerusalem: Believe in the Lord your God, and you shall be established; believe His prophets, and you shall prosper." And when he had consulted with the people, he appointed those who should sing to the Lord, and who should praise the beauty of holiness, as they went out before the army and were saying: "Praise the Lord, For His mercy endures forever." Now when they began to sing and to praise, the Lord set ambushes against the people of Ammon,

Moab, and Mount Seir, who had come against Judah; and they were defeated.

2 Chronicles 20:20–22 (NKJV)

Praises to God bring down His presence and makes Him to show His almightiness. All enemies must bow to the praise of God! There are numerous other examples in the Bible. Go read about Paul and Silas worshipping their way out of prison chains or the falling of the wall of Jericho because of shouts of praise. The Bible says we are created to bring pleasure to God. But only those who belong to God can touch Him by praise. Sin will stop you from praising Him. So repent and get your praise on. Are you ready to praise your way through the storm?

Jesus, I am ready to trust You through this storm, and I want to praise You. In Jesus' name.

Amen.

DAY 57:

"Overflow"

"I pray that God, the source of hope, will fill you completely with joy and peace because you trust in him. Then you will overflow with confident hope through the power of the Holy Spirit."

Romans 15:13 (NLT)

Have you noticed there has been a change in the atmosphere lately? I sat by the ocean, hearing the rumbling of the waves, and I heard Jesus say so plainly to me, "I am about to stir the waters and break something." Lord, what does that mean? He said, "A tsunami of My spirit is coming!" I can see the Lord is trying to prepare us for something bigger than us. I trust completely in His plans for my life. As I read Genesis 7:11 (NKJV), it says, "In the six hundredth year of Noah's life, in the second month, the seventeenth day of the month, on that day all the fountains of the great deep were broken up, and the windows of heaven were opened."

What comes to mind when I say the word overflow? What does that mean to you? The word "overflow" in the King James Version is abound. This word in Greek means "to superabound" (in quantity or quality). So, because you trust in Him, He will cause you to superabound with hope. Oh my goodness, friend, doesn't that make you hunger and thirst for that kind of hope? It brings to mind, for me, the verse in John 7:38 (NKJV), "He who believes in Me, as the Scripture has said, out of his heart will flow rivers of living water." This, my friend, is a superabundance of God's grace, His mercy, and His deep, deep love for you, and it's all flowing from inside of you. It comes pouring out of your heart. Oh, what a treasure! King Solomon said it best in Proverbs 4:23 (NASB), "Watch over your heart with all diligence, for from it flow the springs of life."

I hope you can see by now that the heart is the center of life. The heart is the seat of emotion. It is the center of the will. It represents the whole inner being of mankind and who he is. It is the true self. The true self or true life is not just something you have. Life wells up as truth is made one's own and then flows out. This is why the Lord tells us to guard our heart with all diligence. Our heart is the very core of who we are, and the enemy wants nothing more than to steal your heart. If Satan can get your heart, then he has taken your true identity. He will toy with your heart and cause you to drift with the wind.

But Jesus is the anchor of your soul (see Hebrews 6:19). You get through the storm when the anchor holds you, not when you hold it. So when the storm is raging and the tempest is blowing, allow Jesus to be your anchor. He will hold you fast and keep you from drifting. He knows your name, and He knows every aspect and dimension of your character. He is your creator after all. No one knows you better than Jesus. He knows how to handle the storms in your life, and He knows what will satisfy your needs. All we need to do is ask Him.

I remember a time I sat next to the ocean asking God for a rhema word, and He said *deep*. As you study the word "deep" in Hebrew, it means "literally deep," but in Greek it means "great deep." God is shifting the atmosphere, and He is about to open heaven for us! We need to learn how to lean into what He is doing and be very obedient in whatever He asks us to do! We should be in our Bibles daily and running after Him like we never have before. Seeking His face and not His hand! He says in Isaiah 43:19 (NKJV), "Behold, I will do a new thing, now it shall spring forth; Shall you not know it? I will even make a road in the wilderness and rivers in the desert." Friends, are you putting your trust in our precious Jesus, or are you letting the world dictate your life? The answer is Jesus! The answer is in His nailed, scarred hands and feet! Just bow down to Him and give Him *all* of you! He is waiting! Are you ready for the overflow in your life?

Jesus, I am ready to go deeper into Your Word and Your will for my life. Teach me to accept the overflow You have for my life. In Jesus' name. Amen.

DAY 58:

"The Joy of the Lord Is Your Strength"

And Nehemiah, who was the governor, Ezra the priest and scribe, and the Levites who taught the people said to all the people, "This day is holy to the Lord your God; do not mourn nor weep." For all the people wept, when they heard the words of the Law. Then he said to them, "Go your way, eat the fat, drink the sweet, and send portions to those for whom nothing is prepared; for this day is holy to our Lord. Do not sorrow, for the joy of the Lord is your strength." So the Levites quieted all the people, saying, "Be still, for the day is holy; do not be grieved."

Nehemiah 8:9–11 (NKJV)

Strength only comes when our eyes stay on Christ from where our help comes from. I am reminded of the story of Peter walking on water in Matthew 14:22–33, where Jesus had commanded Him to come to Him on the water. The story occurs right after Jesus fed the five thousand with five loaves of bread and two fish. After feeding the five thousand, the disciples cleaned up the area and picked up twelve baskets full of leftovers. After cleaning up, Jesus sent His disciples to the other side of the sea while He went up on the mountain to pray. It was evening time, and the hour was getting late when Jesus started His journey to the other side of the sea. One difference was Jesus didn't take the long way around the sea or take a boat; no, Jesus took off walking on the water in the middle of a storm. The boat was being tossed to and fro, but Jesus just kept walking. He started to get close to the boat the disciples were in, traveling across the sea, being tossed about by the waves and the wind. They look up and see a figure of a man walking on the water. Honestly, if I had seen a man walking on the water, I probably would have freaked out just like they did. They thought He was a ghost. Jesus simply said as calmly as He could, "Be of good cheer! It is I; do not be afraid" (Matthew 14:27, NKJV). Peter said, "Oh yeah, if it's really You, tell me to come out to You" (my paraphrase). Jesus said, "Come." Peter got out of the boat keeping His eyes on Jesus until he got afraid because of the wind and the waves. Then he started sinking into the water. Jesus reached down and caught him and pulled Peter out of the water. Jesus said to Peter, "O you of little faith, why did you doubt?" (Matthew 14:31, NKJV). They got back in the boat, and the wind suddenly stopped.

Do you get the feeling that walking on the water in the middle of the storm was a test for Peter? It sure seems like it since the storm stopped right after they got back in the boat. But not only did that single event increase Peter's faith, but it also caused the other disciples to take notice and finally believe that Jesus was Lord…the Son of God. All of Jesus' tests for His people not only address something specific in our life, but the tests also address something else in people around us. His tests are always multifaceted. You might even say Jesus was the ultimate multitasker.

It was the same kind of situation for the Israelites in Nehemiah 8. The Word of God was doing its intended work. Second Timothy 3:16 tells us the Word of God is profitable for reproof and correction. Sometimes it hurts to receive correction, and that's precisely why they were weeping. The joy of the Lord is your strength, even when you are being corrected. The people were sad because they were aware of their sin. But they could walk in joy because God was doing a mighty work.

So, even when we are walking through great storms in our life, we can trust in Him because it will be joyful when the storm is over. The conviction of our sin will increase our faith and take us to the other side of our pain and suffering. The process is painful; going through the storm instead of avoiding the storm is never what we want to do. But if we choose to be obedient and keep our eyes on Christ, from where our strength comes, then He will lead us to the other side in peace.

Think about the situation you may be going through right now. You lost a baby, and the pain is unbearable at times. But what happens when you are rewarded for your faith and are blessed with a rainbow baby? You haven't forgotten about the pain of losing your first baby, but the joy of your rainbow baby suddenly outweighs the pain. Joy always comes in the morning. You might even be able to say joy comes through the mourning. The pain will begin to fade, but not the memory of your loved one. You will have joy that comes from the Lord. That is the best kind of joy, and it beats happiness any day. Can you say the joy of the Lord is your strength?

Jesus, I want my pain to turn into joy. I need Your strength to handle this and to walk through it. I pray for the joy of the Lord to enter my heart right here and now. In Jesus' name. Amen.

DAY 59:

"Beautifully Broken"

Yet when holy lovers of God cry out to him with all their hearts, the Lord will hear them and come to rescue them from all their troubles. The Lord is close to all whose hearts are crushed by pain, and he is always ready to restore the repentant one. Even when bad things happen to the good and godly ones, the Lord will save them and not let them be defeated by what they face. God will be your bodyguard to protect you when trouble is near. Not one bone will be broken.

Psalm 34:17–20 (TPT)

The pain inside a heart that has been broken can only be healed by Jesus. But what does this look like, my friends? Let's look at some examples from the Bible.

There was an event that took place in the life of Jesus that He said should be told whenever the gospel is proclaimed around the world. It was when Mary of Bethany came and anointed Him with the perfume, which cost a year's wages. It was an extravagant act of sacrificial worship, and the aroma of it filled the room. Jesus was profoundly moved by it.[12]

Though the men gathered there were indignant, Jesus said, "She has done a beautiful thing to Me." It was a woman who did this for Christ. She knew what she was doing without knowing.

Just as it was also a woman who rushed into the Pharisee's house uninvited and washed Jesus' feet with her tears, dried them with her hair, and kissed them in an act of intimate, repentant worship. It was women who followed Jesus from Galilee to care for His needs. It was women who stayed at the foot of the cross, offering Him the comfort of their presence until He breathed His last.

It was to women that Jesus first revealed Himself after He rose from the dead. Women hold a special place in the heart of God. A woman's worship brings Jesus immense pleasure and a deep ministry. You can minister to the heart of God. You affect Him. You matter. Jesus desires you to pour out your love on Him in extravagant worship. This is not just for women who have the time, women who are really spiritual. You are made for romance, and the only One who can offer it to you consistently and deeply is Jesus. Offer your heart to Him![13]

It is to the broken-hearted that God is most drawn to. God is attracted by need. He wants us to ask

---

12 "The Daily Memo | May 27, 2022 | Offer Your Heart," Embracing Brokenness Ministries, https://embracingbrokenness.org/2022/05/the-daily-memo-may-27-2022-offer-your-heart/.

13 Embracing Brokenness Ministries, "The Daily Memo | May 27, 2022 | Offer Your Heart."

for help to release our cares to Him so that He can go to work on our behalf. But the problem is the people in their brokenness often don't see God as the source of their help or the healer of their soul. Charles Spurgeon put this way, "Broken hearts think God is far away, when He is really most near to them; their eyes are holden so that they see not their best friend. Indeed, He is with them, and in them but they know it not."

Men tend to push back their emotions when emotionally broken. They push back the pain instead of dealing with it. Women, on the other hand, are able to express their pain and share their troubles with each other more effectively. Men rarely, if ever, will share their feelings with one another. In times of loss men will turn to work or meaningless activities to keep their mind off the pain. Where women will consult with each other and talk out their problems. I believe that is why Jesus was drawn to the needs of women who were in pain. The men of that time just didn't admit any kind of weakness and often expressed their pain through anger and lashing out at the innocent. The reality is that not much has changed over time. Men still do this today.

Everybody, men and women alike, must be able to talk about their wounds in a healthy, nonjudgmental way. But mostly, we all need to take our problems to Jesus and truly and honestly express what we are going through. The truth is…He already knows anyway, but He is a gentleman and will not intervene where He is not invited. So invite Him, and He will heal your heart in His time and in His way. Can you submit your wound to Jesus and leave it with Him?

Jesus, help me pour out all the hurts and wounds upon You. I know I can't do this alone. Come, Jesus, and fill me with what only You can provide. In Jesus' mighty name. Amen.

DAY 60:

"I Want to Fall into Your Hands"

"Fear not, for I am with you; Be not dismayed, for I am your God. I will strengthen you, Yes, I will help you, I will uphold you with My righteous right hand."

Isaiah 41:10(NKJV)

Folks, bad things happen to good people. Many of us have had a tragic situation or a close call, and we've said something along the lines, "God, I'm sorry for what I've done, but please don't hurt my child," or maybe "Please don't take my husband, wife, or child." The truth is some of us have been raised under bad theology. I'm here to tell you straight up God did not take your baby from you. God did not split up your marriage. God is not punishing you for some mistake you may have made. Do we receive discipline or instruction for when we do something wrong? Of course, every good father disciplines his child for the child's good, not for the child's harm.

I want you to notice something in today's scripture. In the latter half of Isaiah 41:10, and these are the words of the Father Himself, notice He says, "Yes, I will help you." But let's take a look at more of chapter 41; God tells us in verse 9 that He has chosen us and has not cast us away. Just before He tells us that He will help us, He says He will strengthen us, and just after He offers His help, He says, "I will uphold you with My righteous right hand." (In Scripture, the right hand is the hand of power.) In verses 11 and 12 He says that He is going to come against those who attempt to harm us. In verse 13 He says again that He is going to hold our right hand and help us, "I will help you." Lastly, in verse 14, He goes on to tell us despite our sin (when He is talking about Jacob being a worm, He is referring to sin…He's not calling the House of Jacob, Israel, a name) right after this He says, "I will help you." In the matter of five verses in Isaiah 41, God tells us that He will help us three times in this passage. If you have studied the Bible, then you know that repetition is hugely important…it means that what He is saying is of extreme importance, and you had better take notice of what word or phrase is being repeated. He loves us, and He wants to help us!

But there is an issue that must be dealt with, and few people who read the Bible only at a surface level will take notice of it. God is the God of law and order. God will not violate His own law or His promises. Psalm 115:16 (NKJV) talks about this, "The heaven, even the heavens, are the Lord's; But *the earth He has given to the children of men*" (emphasis mine). In Genesis, the rule of the earth was first established as belonging to mankind. Read Genesis 1:26–28 (NKJV):

> *Then God said, "Let Us make man in Our image, according to Our likeness; let them have dominion over the fish of the sea, over the birds of the air, and over the cattle, over all the earth and over every creeping thing that creeps on the earth." So God created man in His own image; in the image of God He created him; male and female He created them. Then God blessed them, and God said to them, "Be fruitful and multiply; fill the earth and subdue it; have dominion over the fish of the sea, over the birds of the air, and over every living thing that moves on the earth." (emphasis mine).*

Basically, the word "dominion" means "to rule over." But in chapter 3 of Genesis, mankind handed over their authority over the earth to Satan during the fall of man.

God will not and cannot interfere with the rulership of the earth because He gave it to us to manage and rule over. God is a gentleman and a promise keeper, not a promise breaker. When we try to blame God for something that He has clearly given us authority over, it's like saying to the government, "We voted you into office to rule over us, and now we don't like the laws that you have created on our behalf." We have no one to blame but ourselves because we voted for our governmental representatives. It's the same with God; He gave us the ability to govern our own world. We are the ones who totally messed up what He has given us authority over, and we want to blame Him. We have handcuffed God by our sins and by the fact that we won't invite Him into our lives to take lordship. When we surrender our will to Him, then He can act on our behalf. So let's take a closer look at a scenario that some may be enduring right now. Let's say you and your husband have been trying to get pregnant for years with no success, or maybe you have gotten pregnant but miscarried shortly after getting pregnant. Do you blame God for your situation? Let's take a closer look. Maybe you also gossip about your neighbors or your family while trying to get pregnant. Or you are a believer, but your husband is not a believer. Maybe you attend church whenever you "feel" like it. You have accepted Jesus Christ as your Savior, but you have had zero transformation…you look just like a nonbeliever to your neighbors. All of these situations are a violation of God's Word. Let's call it what it is…*sin*. Can you expect the blessings of God while you are living in sin? I am not talking about an occasional screwup. I am talking about a pattern of habitual sin in your life that you refuse to address. God will not bless a mess. He expects a transformation when we accept Jesus as Savior. Accepting Jesus is just the first step in a long, long journey. The Word says, "Enter by the narrow gate; for wide is the gate and broad is the way that leads to destruction, and there are many who go in by it. Because narrow is the gate and difficult is the way which leads to life, and there are few who find it" (Matthew 7:13–14, NKJV).

The Christian life is a journey, but Jesus has traveled the road ahead of us to point us to the path. Without Jesus the road to righteousness is impassible. But with Him, we are given the tools we need to rule well, to manage His kingdom and call it down to earth. Invite His kingdom to come into your situation. Invite the Holy Spirit into your day every day. Remember we have a role to play on this earth, and it is a significant role. It is vital, however, that we allow His Spirit to direct our path and lead us in the way we should go. The Father wants the absolute best for us, but sometimes we have to accept His correction to put us on the right path for our lives. We cannot take matters into our own hands and expect to get a divine outcome. He will not answer prayers of those who are consciously living in sin. Get your life in alignment with Him, and He will direct your path. Will it be easy? *No!* Will it be worth it? Absolutely, yes! If something bad has happened to you and you're blaming God, ask yourself, *Have I done something to open the door that allowed the enemy to come in?*

Father, help me look at myself and see if there are any wicked ways with me. Wash me white as soon and make me new! I love You, Lord, and I want to make You my Lord. In Jesus' name.

Amen.

DAY 61:

"The Lord Is My Light"

"Do not rejoice over me, my enemy; When I fall, I will arise; When I sit in darkness, The Lord will be a light to me."

Micah 7:8 (NKJV)

There have been times in my life when I felt as though the enemies were throwing parties to watch wave after wave of calamities hit my life. Our trials and storms can feel like a never-ending story. But the Lord always has the final say. This verse from Micah 7 clearly says to my enemies, "You had better be careful because this child of Mine will arise out of the dust heap, and I will be her light." Light always overcomes darkness. There has never been an instance where darkness wins over light. My enemies may see me brought low for a moment, but they should know that I won't be low for long. My God will lift me up!

This verse also draws me to another more well-known passage in Psalm 23:

Yea, though I walk through the valley of the shadow of death, I will fear no evil; For You are with me; Your rod and Your staff, they comfort me. You prepare a table before me in the presence of my enemies; You anoint my head with oil; My cup runs over. Surely goodness and mercy shall follow me All the days of my life; And I will dwell in the house of the Lord Forever.

Psalm 23:4–6 (NKJV)

Did you catch the part about God preparing a table for you in the presence of your enemies? As you thrive and prosper, God will set a table of the finest meal, and your enemies will be forced to watch you. This will be the ultimate defeat for that loser—the devil. The people he was trying to destroy and separate from God will now dine with the Father while they have to watch the whole thing knowing they will be sent to the pit and eternal damnation.

The Lord is my light and my salvation—so why should I be afraid? The Lord is my fortress, protecting me from danger, so why should I tremble? When evil people come to devour me, when my enemies and foes attack me, they will stumble and fall. Though a mighty army surrounds me, my heart will not be afraid. Even if I am attacked, I will remain confident.

Psalm 27:1–3 (NLT)

I hope and pray you are catching the theme here. For those of us who are walking as children of the light, the Lord will make sure of our safety and give us protection from our enemies. In fact, He will make sure we rise above our circumstances to a great victory. The truth is the war is over; there are only small battles left to fight. Jesus has already obtained the victory for us.

My father-in-law used to say, "It's okay to get knocked down, but don't stay down. Rise up on your feet, dust yourself off, and put one foot in front of the other." That's what fighting the good fight looks like sometimes. Victory comes when we don't allow the enemy to see us down. The only time the enemy should ever see us down is when we are on our knees, and then he should start sweating. As one of my granddaughters says, he should just go home and cry about it. Now that Papa God is involved, he stands no chance at bringing his darkness over my life. The light of His glory destroys all darkness. Speaking of His glory, I can add that it says in Revelation 21:23–24 (TPT), "The city has no need for the sun or moon to shine, for the glory of God is its light, and its lamp is the Lamb. The people will walk by its light and the kings of the earth will bring their wealth into it." Can you imagine? Think about that. God is the only light in heaven. No sun, no moon, only His glory.

The only time you should be in darkness is in your secret place with your face on the ground crying out to God. You may be in a lot of pain from the blows the enemy has inflicted upon you. You may not see a way out of the darkness. Stay in your secret place and fight the good fight. Stay in your secret place and wait for Him to move you out. Stand strong in the face of opposition and continue landing punches on the enemy's nose. You are victorious through Jesus Christ, and you can do all things through Him, who gives you strength. Jesus said in John 14:6 that He is the way and the truth and the life; no one comes to the Father except through Him. And Jesus has said that the Father is in Him and He is in the Father. So, if this is true, then the glory of the Father is in Jesus too. Follow the light of Jesus Christ and walk straight into the arms of the Father. He is waiting for you. In the midst of the darkness all around you, can you see the glory of God to lead you home?

Jesus, help me see You in everything around me and let me see Your glory! In Jesus' name.

Amen.

DAY 62:

"Whom Shall I Fear?"

The Lord is my light and my salvation; Whom shall I fear? The Lord is the strength of my life; Of whom shall I be afraid? When the wicked came against me To eat up my flesh, My enemies and foes, They stumbled and fell. Though an army may encamp against me, My heart shall not fear; Though war may rise against me, In this I will be confident. One thing I have desired of the Lord, That will I seek: That I may dwell in the house of the Lord All the days of my life, To behold the beauty of the Lord, And to inquire in His temple. For in the time of trouble He shall hide me in His pavilion; In the secret place of His tabernacle He shall hide me; He shall set me high upon a rock. And now my head shall be lifted up above my enemies all around me; Therefore I will offer sacrifices of joy in His tabernacle; I will sing, yes, I will sing praises to the Lord. Hear, O Lord, when I cry with my voice! Have mercy also upon me, and answer me. When You said, "Seek My face," My heart said to You, "Your face, Lord, I will seek." Do not hide Your face from me; Do not turn Your servant away in anger; You have been my help; Do not leave me nor forsake me, O God of my salvation. When my father and my mother forsake me, Then the Lord will take care of me. Teach me Your way, O Lord, And lead me in a smooth path, because of my enemies. Do not deliver me to the will of my adversaries; For false witnesses have risen against me, And such as breathe out violence. I would have lost heart, unless I had believed That I would see the goodness of the Lord In the land of the living. Wait on the Lord; Be of good courage, And He shall strengthen your heart; Wait, I say, on the Lord!

Psalm 27:1–14 (NKJV)

As I was reading Psalm 27, I was reminded that King David was a man after God's own heart! He was a worshiper and not a worrier! He knew God on an intimate level, so he would praise and worship his way through all stages in life, the good and the bad. David had everything a man could want in life. He had wealth, power, authority, respect, and adoration. He faced many enemies and battles throughout his life, but he always knew where his help came from! Like many of the psalms written by David, Psalm 27 was written during a season of trouble. Yet Psalm 27 is not like a tragedy written by Shakespeare; it's a song of triumph over darkness. The Lord was David's light and salvation.

David didn't despair in darkness. In fact, I would say that David embraced the darkness. It was when David couldn't see that all his faith was put in God. His life was filled with light because of God. So

151

how about you? Are you dwelling in darkness because Jesus is your light? Trust Him through everything, even in the darkest hours of your life. He will make a way where there seems to be no way. When you've tried everything to find healing and hope again but just can't seem to make any headway, turn to Christ. When you've read every self-help book and listened to countless TED Talks or podcasts, turn to Jesus. He is the source of your hope and healing.

You see, to experience spiritual intimacy with Jesus, you must seek Him! Read Jeremiah 29:13. "If we rarely know what it is to have God be the strength of our life, perhaps it is because we trust in so many other things for strength, instead of the source of our strength. We find it easy to trust in our wisdom, our experience, our friends, and our resources."[14] But David knew a strength greater than all these things because he put his faith in God, who is the source of all strength. David, too, had to give a baby back to God. David's son was the product of the sin that he committed with Bathsheba, but he fasted and prayed for seven days to save his son. Once he knew that there was nothing else he could do and that the loss was inevitable, David ate. (See 2 Samuel 12:23.)

I'm not saying that you lost your child as a result of some sin in your life. But I am saying you can take a page out of David's story and repent of any sin that you may have in your life, then move on in service to God. David was able to recover and find healing in his intimate relationship with the Lord. David understood that when his child died, his son's spirit was released from his body and carried in the arms of an angel to rest with the righteous spirits that paved the way ahead of him into Abraham's bosom because Jesus had not yet gone to the cross. He knew he could not bring his son back to life, but he knew he would join his son again one day in paradise.

Myself, I find it very helpful to find a place where I can be alone with Him, a secret place or a room in my home (I have a prayer closet) where I can have quiet and stillness, just me and the Lord. I would encourage you today to find your place and sit quietly with Him. It's not about long-winded prayers to God. In fact, sometimes He just wants you to sit with Him. The best treasure is often found in darkness. Let Him speak to your heart and heal any areas that might need some healing! He wants spiritual intimacy with you! He's waiting for you. Have you found your secret place to be alone with God?

Father God, help me to trust You when things look so dark. Teach me to lean into Your understanding and help me find the quietness my soul longs for so desperately. Oh, how I need You, Jesus. Amen.

---

14 "Psalm 27—the Seeking, Waiting Life Rewarded," in David Guzik, *The Enduring Word Bible Commentary* (2020), https://enduringword.com/bible-commentary/psalm-27/.

DAY 63:

"I Want Everything I Do to Point to Jesus"

"Keep creating in me a clean heart. Fill me with pure thoughts and holy desires, ready to please you."

Psalm 51:10 (TPT)

It's funny how the life we expect seems to never turn out the way we planned it. As young ladies we want to get married to our handsome prince, have the house with the white picket fence, and have a family, but sometimes things don't quite turn out that way.

We find out the prince charming has a problem with alcohol, or the mother-in-law is not as loving as we had hoped for, or we find out that we are having trouble getting pregnant. This is where the enemy comes in. The Bible tells us in Ephesians 6:12 (NKJV), "For we do not wrestle against flesh and blood, but against principalities, against powers, against the rulers of the darkness of this age, against spiritual hosts of wickedness in the heavenly places." So this tells me…we have a real enemy that we cannot see with the naked eye. We have to learn to stand on His Word to get ourselves through these tough times, but it can only be done with Christ. The Word says, "Trust in the Lord with all your heart, And lean not on your own understanding; In all your ways acknowledge Him, And He shall direct your paths. Do not be wise in your own eyes; Fear the Lord and depart from evil" (Proverbs 3:5–7, NKJV). His Word is a lamp to our feet and a light to our path (Psalm 119:105). We must learn how to lean on Jesus and hear His voice and obey His commands for our victory! We *are* in the army of God, and we do have a commanding officer in Jesus Christ. We must obey Him in order to be victorious!

Life can throw you one trial after another, but how you walk it out with Jesus tells a lot about you. Life with Christ is not all roses—trust me—the enemy comes at me faster than I could imagine sometimes, and he always slithers through the back door. He will not knock on your door and be polite. You won't see him pull up on your ring doorbell. He is cunning in all his ways and slithers around like a snake, or as it says in 1 Peter 5:8 (NKJV), "Be sober, be vigilant; because your adversary the devil walks about like a roaring lion, seeking whom he may devour." He is walking about pretending to be a lion… he's not a lion. There's only one Lion of Judah, and that is Jesus Christ. But the enemy will stalk you and push the buttons that lead you down the wrong path. *Be careful* then how you live and the voices that you listen to.

People have asked me many times how you know when it's the voice of God talking to you. Well, first of all, anything Jesus tells me will line up with His Word. The enemy is loud, and he tells you lies. Satan is able to make lies look like the truth and unbelievers look like believers. He is so good at using God's Word—just enough to make you think it's truth. Satan knows the Word of God better than you do, and he will take it out of context to suit his needs and desires. He will use snippets of the Word to entice you and bait you so he can put his hook into you. One key point is the enemy will often attempt to use these snippets to condemn us, not edify us. But Romans 8:1 (NKJV) says, "There is therefore now no condemnation to those who are in Christ Jesus, who do not walk according to the flesh, but according to the Spirit."

A mother who has lost a baby may hear something like this at a time of weakness, "Your baby's death is because of you. You caused it all. You didn't eat right; you didn't get enough exercise; you didn't follow the doctor's orders." The enemy waits for an opportune time to attack. He is always condemning or enticing. He wants you to live out of your fleshly desires. If you are in Christ Jesus, you must walk according to the Spirit who lives within you. There are times when you have to tell the devil to leave you alone, to stop speaking lies to you, and you have to declare the Scriptures back to him. This is why it is imperative to have a thorough understanding of the Word. "My people are destroyed for lack of knowledge. Because you have rejected knowledge, I also will reject you from being priest for Me; Because you have forgotten the law of your God, I also will forget your children" (Hosea 4:6, NKJV). When you know Scripture and can rightly divide it using it in its proper context, you have a weapon in your arsenal that cannot be beaten by the enemy.

When the enemy comes, he does not come to play or sow blessings; he comes to sow bad things into your life (Matthew 13:24–25). He isn't going to make what he sows sound like he will destroy you. But that is his main goal. Satan hates you, and he hates the Spirit inside of you. Why does he hate us so much that he seeks to destroy us? Because we bear the image of our Creator, and He gave us the right to be like Him. This doesn't mean we are God or can be our own god. It means through the blood of Jesus Christ, we are image bearers and have been given an inheritance that includes the full authority of Jesus Christ in heaven and on this earth. We are sons and daughters of the Lord God Almighty because of the blood covenant. We have full access to all the weapons of warfare and the full rights of a child of God. We must believe we have the power and authority, and we must wield it correctly. But remember this one thing—the blood is enough! Have you exercised your power and authority as a child of God?

Jesus, I know the enemy will come after me, but I am pleading Your blood over my life and my family because I know You are enough. In Jesus' name. Amen.

DAY 64:

"Kingly Desire"

"So the King will greatly desire your beauty; Because He is your Lord, worship Him."

Psalm 45:11(NKJV)

I keep hearing the Lord say, "Be holy because I am holy." Scripture tells us, "But as He who called you is holy, you also be holy in all your conduct, because it is written, "Be holy, for I am holy" (1 Peter 1:15–16, NKJV). Lord, can I be holy? What does this look like? "He" reminds me in 1 Thessalonians 4:7 (NKJV), "For God did not call us to uncleanness, but in holiness," and then in Hebrews 12:14 (NKJV), "Pursue peace with all people, and holiness, without which no one will see the Lord." The definition of "holiness" is "a state of being holy." So, as I think of what "holy" means, I know it is dedication or consecration to Adonai. I must hold "Him" above all things. He is sacred and to be treasured! My dear friends, do you see God this way? Is "He" first in your life? Do you speak to "Him" as you wake up and as you go to sleep? I would encourage you to seek "Him" in such a way that the entire world you live in…sees "Him" first! "He" is worthy of all our praise and worship!

I am also reminded of what holiness looks like when I read 1 Thessalonians 5:15–24 (NKJV):

> *See that no one renders evil for evil to anyone, but always pursue what is good both for yourselves and for all. pray without ceasing, in everything give thanks; for this is the will of God in Christ Jesus for you. Rejoice always, Do not quench the Spirit. Do not despise prophecies. Test all things; hold fast what is good. Abstain from every form of evil. Now may the God of peace Himself sanctify you completely; and may your whole spirit, soul, and body be preserved blameless at the coming of our Lord Jesus Christ. He who calls you is faithful, who also will do it.*

Holiness is being set apart from the world. We are to be in the world, not of it. We must keep in mind that from Him we came and to Him we shall return. In the meantime, we are to live a life that draws people to Him; we are to seek to live a biblical life.

I hate it when I hear people say something like, "We can't live biblically nowadays. It's a different world from when the Bible was written. There are gray areas in the Bible." All of that is nothing but hogwash! The Bible says we are to be like Jesus in the way we live. In 1 Thessalonians 5:23 it says God will sanctify us. Sanctification means purifying us externally, the way we look and act on the outside, and then He purifies us by redemption, giving us freedom from the guilt of sin, and thirdly, He purifies us internally by renewing of the soul; the old man is dead, and the new man lives eternally. Sanctification is a purification and a consecration from the world. We are truly set apart.

Does being holy mean we are to live a perfect, sinless life? No, there has only been one perfect man on this earth, the man Jesus Christ. We can't live a perfect life, but we are to strive for it. Jesus died so that we don't have to live a perfect, sinless life. That should be the Christian's goal. But this is a goal we will never be able to achieve. However, that doesn't mean we can't work toward that goal. In so doing, we will peel back the onion layers of our life, peeling back the wicked parts of us one layer at a time. After all, it says in Luke 13:24 (NKJV) to "strive to enter through the narrow gate." Unless you work hard to remove the baggage that is holding you back, you will never be able to enter through the narrow gate.

What's holding you back? Is it unforgiveness over an offense? Maybe it's a lie you've been living. Or maybe you have pride in life. Maybe you can't forgive God for your child who passed away. Whatever it is that is holding you back from being all that God wants you to be, release it, give it over to Him, and seek to live a life of holiness. The list provided in 1 Thessalonians 5 is pretty extensive but not impossible. Being holy creates something beautiful from your life that draws that Lord to you. In Psalm 45:11 it says the king will greatly desire your beauty. That's what comes from living a holy life. Will you make mistakes and fall? Absolutely, then you repent, ask for forgiveness quickly, and you move on to the next day. So what do you think? Can you live a life of holiness?

King Jesus, help me to live a life of holiness and consecration where You will desire my beauty, Lord. Come, Jesus, Your daughter awaits You. In Jesus' name. Amen.

DAY 65:

"The Anointing at Bethany"

And being in Bethany at the house of Simon the leper, as He sat at the table, a woman came having an alabaster flask of very costly oil of spikenard. Then she broke the flask and poured it on His head. But there were some who were indignant among themselves, and said, "Why was this fragrant oil wasted? For it might have been sold for more than three hundred denarii and given to the poor." And they criticized her sharply. But Jesus said, "Let her alone. Why do you trouble her? She has done a good work for Me. For you have the poor with you always, and whenever you wish you may do them good; but Me you do not have always. She has done what she could. She has come beforehand to anoint My body for burial. Assuredly, I say to you, wherever this gospel is preached in the whole world, what this woman has done will also be told as a memorial to her."

Mark 14:3–9(NKJV)

As stated in day 59,

> there was an event that took place in the life of Jesus that He said should be told whenever the gospel is proclaimed around the world. It was when Mary of Bethany came and anointed Him with the perfume, which cost a year's wages. It was an extravagant act of sacrificial worship, and the aroma of it filled the room. Jesus was profoundly moved by it.[15]

Though the men gathered there were indignant, Jesus said, "She has done a beautiful thing to me." It was a woman who did this for Christ.

> Just as it was also a woman who rushed into the Pharisee's house uninvited and washed Jesus' feet with her tears, dried them with her hair, and kissed them in an act of intimate, repentant worship. It was women who followed Jesus from Galilee to care for His needs. It was women who stayed at the foot of the cross, offering Him the comfort of their presence until He breathed His last.

> It was to women that Jesus first revealed Himself after He rose from the dead. Women hold a special place in the heart of God. A woman's worship brings Jesus immense pleasure and a deep ministry. You can minister to the heart of God. You affect Him. You matter. Jesus desires you to pour out your love on Him in extravagant worship. This is not just for women who have the time, women who are really spiritual. You are made for romance, and the only

15 Embracing Brokenness Ministries, "The Daily Memo | May 27, 2022 | Offer Your Heart."

One who can offer it to you consistently and deeply is Jesus. Offer your heart to Him![16]

When was the last time you were at the feet of Jesus? Just broken before "Him," tears pouring out as you look toward "Him" for help (Psalm 56:8). Mary knew this all too well…she knew where her help came from (Psalm 121:1–2)! "And certain women who had been healed of evil spirits and infirmities—Mary called Magdalene, out of whom had come seven demons" (Luke 8:2, NKJV). Do you think because He delivered her from demons she lay at His feet? Or because she loved Him? I love this verse in Mark 16:9 where Jesus chooses to appear to Mary Magdalene first! Jesus chose to appear *first* to Mary… He chose the one the world had discarded! That should give you so much *hope*, my friends! Jesus Christ of Nazareth chose to appear to a former demon-possessed woman who was a prostitute!

Mary of Bethany and Mary Magdalene are both stories of triumph over tragedy. Mary of Bethany had lost her brother Lazarus, and Jesus rose him from the dead. Mary Magdalene was possessed by demons before Jesus delivered her. Both ladies didn't dwell on their circumstances but had heard about the One who could change their lives forever. They wholeheartedly sought after Him because of what they had heard. These women were delivered from their circumstances by the only One who could truly help them. Others may have tried to help these women, but only Jesus could heal them completely. As a result of what Jesus did for them, they extravagantly worshipped Jesus for the Savior that He is. He will bring healing and restoration, but you must trust Him wholeheartedly. Do you have the kind of faith in Jesus to trust Him amid your most dire of circumstances?

God, I pour out my love in heartfelt worship to You! Show me how to love You in extravagant ways! In Jesus' name…amen!

---

16 Embracing Brokenness Ministries, "The Daily Memo | May 27, 2022 | Offer Your Heart."

DAY 66:

"Comfort in the Morning"

"God blesses those people who grieve. They will find comfort!"

Matthew 5:4 (CEV)

In biblical times having a multitude of children was considered a sign of fruitfulness, blessing, and favor of the Lord. Psalm 127:3–5 (TPT) describes the blessing of children like this:

> *Children are God's love-gift; they are heaven's generous reward. Children born to a young couple will one day rise to protect and provide for their parents. Happy will be the couple who has many of them! A household full of children will not bring shame on your name but victory when you face your enemies, for your offspring will have influence and honor to prevail on your behalf!*

But what about the couples who are unable to get pregnant or who have great difficulty getting pregnant? In the Scriptures there are many examples of this exact situation. I can't list them all in this short devotional, but I will give you three good ones...let's talk about the stories of Sarah, Hannah, and Elizabeth.

In Genesis 17, God made a covenant with Abram. God changed Abram's name to Abraham and promised him that he would be the father of many nations. Then, in Genesis 17:15–16 (NKJV), "Then God said to Abraham, As for Sarai your wife, you shall not call her name Sarai, but Sarah shall be her name. And I will bless her and also give you a son by her; then I will bless her, and she shall be a mother of nations; kings of peoples shall be from her.'" What did Abraham do when God said this to him? Abraham fell on his face and laughed! Can you imagine being seventy-five years old and your wife sixty-five years old and God telling you that you would be the father and mother of many nations? *Wow*...here again, God is the God of the impossible. To make the matter more impossible, they had to wait twenty-five years before the fulfillment of that promise from God. Through Isaac the prophecy for being the father and mother of many nations was fulfilled.

Hannah's story is found in 1 Samuel 1 and 2. She was one of two wives married to a Jewish man named Elkanah. The other wife, named Peninnah, had children, but Hannah was unable to conceive. This grieved Hannah greatly! One year Hannah traveled to the tabernacle located in Shiloh, where she prayed at the entrance of the tabernacle for a child. In 1 Samuel 1:11 (NKJV), *she made a vow and said, "O Lord of hosts, if You will indeed look on the affliction of Your maidservant and remember me, and not forget Your maidservant, but will give Your maidservant a male child, then I will give him to the Lord all the days of his life, and no razor shall come upon his head."*

The high priest of the tabernacle, Eli, saw Hannah praying passionately but silently for a child, and he rebuked her, thinking she was drunk. Hannah explained to Eli that she was praying, and Eli blessed her and asked God to grant her request. She returned home and was able to conceive, naming her son Samuel, which means "I have asked for him from the Lord." There are three important lessons to note from Hannah's story. First, she turned to God in prayer in her time of need. Second, she praised and thanked God when He did answer her prayer. Third, she kept her commitment to the Lord, even though it was difficult. God blessed Hannah beyond what she expected as a result of her faithfulness and trust in Him.

Elizabeth's story begins in Luke 1:

There was in the days of Herod, the king of Judea, a certain priest named Zacharias, of the division of Abijah. His wife was of the daughters of Aaron, and her name was Elizabeth. And they were both righteous before God, walking in all the commandments and ordinances of the Lord blameless. But they had no child, because Elizabeth was barren, and they were both well advanced in years.

Luke 1:5–7 (NKJV)

Zacharias was serving in the temple when the angel Gabriel appeared to him. Gabriel told Zacharias that God had answered his prayers. His wife, Elizabeth, would conceive and have a son whose name was to be John. But Zacharias doubted the promise, and because of his lack of faith, God struck him mute until the time his son would be born. When Zacharias returned home, Elizabeth conceived just as the angel Gabriel had said. Their son, John, would become "John the Baptist," filled with the Holy Spirit, and was the herald proclaiming the Messiah, Jesus Christ.

As you can see, barrenness or old age is no obstacle for God. These are just some of the stories in the Bible. But what is the common thread that links these stories together? Faith and belief in what God is capable of doing. You may be experiencing this "barrenness," and you may be doubting what God can do in your life. Repent for your unbelief, and begin to take hold of the promises of God and speak them out. God will do more than you can ask or imagine. But it may not always look the way you think it will look. Remove any preconceived notions of what an answered prayer looks like to you. Trust God and allow Him to do what only God can do. Do you believe God can do the impossible for you?

Jesus, I pray in times of trouble I can run to You, knowing You will always be there for me with open arms. I love You, Lord. In Jesus' name. Amen.

DAY 67

"Triumph over Two Tragedies"

"'For I know the plans I have for you,' says the Lord. 'They are plans for good and not for disaster, to give you a future and a hope. In those days when you pray, I will listen. If you look for me wholeheartedly, you will find me.'"

Jeremiah 29:11–13 (NLT)

"And we know that in all things God works for the good of those who love him, who have been called according to his purpose" (Romans 8:28, NIV).

I want to tell you a story that plays into the heart of why I am sharing my testimony in this book. A fact that is so crazy to me, but it also confirms the love of our all-knowing God. The author of *Father Gives and Takes Away* was a dear friend of mine through junior high and high school. That is to say we even signed all of our daily notes, "Your bestest friend." And now, years later, we both have not only lost a child but children. He promises in Jeremiah 29:11 (NIV), "'For I know the plans I have for you,' declares the Lord, 'plans to prosper you and not to harm you, plans to give you hope and a future.'" You see, He knew that someday we would find peace and fulfillment in Him, and we would be able to share our stories and healing together. He is an amazing Father who is present in all circumstances—past, present, and future.

Most cannot explain or understand the pain of losing a child, but if you are reading this, I probably do not need to explain it. You have felt or are currently feeling the kind of indescribable pain I am referring to, so we can sit here in silence for a moment… But just know, I write this in reverence of you and of my Lord and Savior.

And this is the theme of my testimony, the all-knowing God is there in the hard and devastating moments, even if we are not ready to see it. Psalm 105:4–5 (NIV) reminds us, "Look to the Lord and his strength; seek his face always. Remember the wonders he has done, his miracles, and the judgments he pronounced." Looking back at all I have endured and the ways He has shown up for me has continued to help me in my healing journey. I can look back and see His hands all over my life, even when I could not see them at the moment.

I do not have an "aha" moment of accepting Jesus. I grew up always believing, but I can say now, over fifty years later, I did not walk closely and listen to Him daily as I do now. And although God began healing and guiding me to the next right step many years ago, I have only recently, with His help, started putting it all together. I lost my secondborn in 1989. My almost six-week-old son, Layne, died of sudden infant death syndrome, also known as SIDS. I was devastated and could not understand how this could happen to me. I was a good mom, and some people did not even want their children. So why did God take my son from me?

Back then, I would have told you that my oldest son saved me from the darkness surrounding me over the next few weeks. I now not only know it was God wrapped in all of those so-called coincidences, but He had a miraculous plan that is still being poured over me today. You see, God's healing became more evident years later after the loss of another one of my children.

Suicide took the life of my firstborn, Evan, in 2021; he was almost thirty-seven years old. It was the most painful moment of my life, but God did not allow me to sit in that pain for long. He showed up in a supernatural way just thirty-six hours after this horrific event. The things I experienced can only be explained by the presence of God himself. It is so difficult for me to describe in such short words. He brought so much clarity and surrounded me with His presence. He spoke words of truth and miraculously put several people in my path to confirm His existence and comfort. He placed answers for me to find that only God could have orchestrated, and He continues to show me the next right step.

Only God can teach joy in pain and suffering, but you must listen and find a way to allow Him to pierce through the grief. He can sustain you and make you whole again, but it starts with us. Romans 5:3–5 (ESV) says:

> Not only that, but we rejoice in our sufferings, knowing that suffering produces endurance, and endurance produces character, and character produces hope, and hope does not put us to shame, because God's love has been poured into our hearts through the Holy Spirit who has been given to us.

It starts with us opening our hearts and letting Him in. I do this by welcoming Him into my morning with a prayer. It can be a simple prayer, as simple as, "I want to hear You, Lord; I want to walk with You, Lord." But then you must be ready to listen and to walk. Are you ready to listen and to walk with God on a daily basis?

> Lord Jesus, help me learn to listen to Your voice and obey whatever You ask me to do. I want to invite You into my pain for complete healing in this area of my life. In Jesus' name. Amen.

DAY 68:

"Be Still and Know"

"Surrender your anxiety. Be still and realize that I am God. I am God above all the nations, and I am exalted throughout the whole earth."

Psalm 46:10 (TPT)

The Lord has been calling us to be still before Him. As I sat quietly and listened to those words, my heart wondered what that actually meant to me. Psalm 46:10 (NKJV) says, "Be still, and know I am God; I will be exalted among the nations, I will be exalted in the earth." He is calling me and you to just be still and know Him more and trust Him with whatever storm we might be in. He is able to handle anything! My dear friends, do you truly believe that? Do you believe that anything you are facing that Jesus Christ is enough? Surrendering everything to Him is how we find peace in the storms and are able to just be still and know He is our *God*! I pray you remember this because He still moves mountains! He is Elohim!

Let's face it—we live in a world that is demanding and one that is constantly bombarding us with business. We live at a furious pace with little concern for the impact on our spirit. We wake up and are on the go from the second the alarm goes off. We are filled with business; for most of us, our lives are out of control. Rarely do we sit still before our God and just sit before Him to experience the life that He gives us. "Be still and know" is not a simple command to sit down and not move; rather, it is more of a rebuke for a restless and turbulent world to "stop it! Come rest with Me. I'm here to bring you peace and rest among all the business of your life." He wants us to stop all our striving and attempting to figure our lives out; He wants us to surrender to Him and acknowledge Him as the most high God. The idea is something like this: "As you know the glory and greatness of God, stop your mouth from arguing with Him or opposing Him. Simply surrender."[17]

Most of us, if we are honest with ourselves, have an addiction to control. We want to control our schedule, our finances, our children, even sometimes we want to control our spouse. But control is an illusion! We don't really have control over anything. Yes, we can make decisions to increase the probability that things will work out in our favor. But the reality is life comes at you fast, and suddenly things can change and completely wreck all your plans. I love that old saying that goes something like…"life

---

17 David Guzik, "Study Guide for Psalm 46," updated August 2022, https://www.blueletterbible.org/comm/guzik_david/study-guide/psalm/psalm-46.cfm.

happens while you're making plans." This is sooo true! So how do you conquer this need for control and the need to be constantly busy? You must make a conscious decision to give everything to God! It is really that simple. Do you make decisions based upon God's guidance and revelation? Do you seek His will on where you go on vacation? What about obeying that little voice inside of you that says, "Don't go home your normal way; take a different route"? Many times, this is the voice of God directing your path because He has a better plan or so you can avoid danger. Have you ever thought about life in these terms? Have you ever questioned what would have happened in your life if you had made a different decision at some fork in the road of your life?

Change your life by changing your schedule. A daily quiet time with Him is all you need. You must know His sovereignty over your life. He wants you to take yourself off the throne of your life and put Him back on the throne. He doesn't want to control every movement in your life, but He does want you to surrender every aspect of your life to Him. When life happens and the unexpected hits us, like the death of a child, a divorce, or job loss, etc., we will have stability because we know who we belong to and how much He cares for us. He brings a peace over our lives and gives us the ability to overcome some of the worst circumstances that life can throw at us. This devil wants to steal life from you…the Bible says in John 10:10, "The thief comes only to steal, kill, and destroy," but Jesus came to give us life and life more abundantly. When we are still before Him, we can trust Him with anything in our life and know that He will work everything out for our good.

This book is designed to lead you on a journey to healing and for you to experience God in the midst of one of the worst times of your life. If you slow your life down and allow Him to take control and submit your schedule, your finances, your relationships, etc. (basically, surrender it all to Him), then He will bring peace and contentment in your life. He is a good, good Father, and He desires to give you good gifts (see James 1:17). I will leave you today with this… "Oh, taste and see that the Lord is good. Blessed is the man who trusts in Him" (Psalm 34:8, NKJV). Have you surrendered all to Him?

Lord, help me to sit quietly with You and just be still before You. I need to hear Your voice. I need You to heal my heart, mind, and emotions. In Jesus' mighty name. Amen.

DAY 69:

"Pray with Faith"

"I pray with great faith for you, because I'm fully convinced that the One who began this gracious work in you will faithfully continue the process of maturing you until the unveiling of our Lord Jesus Christ!"

Philippians 1:6 (TPT)

Paul prayed for the church at Philippi with great faith! The Philippians were great supporters of Paul right from day one. When Paul went to prison and praised his way to freedom, it was the Philippians who were holding a round-the-clock prayer vigil for Paul. He knew God had begun a great work in the Philippians, and he prayed earnestly that he would get to see it through to completion. I love how Charles Spurgeon describes this…"Where is there an instance of God beginning any work and leaving it incomplete?" As a believer in the Lord Jesus Christ, God has begun a great work in you too.

Faith is built in the trials of our life. Trials such as when your baby is born a little too early or is born sick. The medical team rushes your baby into the neonatal intensive care unit (NICU) while you are left alone to pray your baby will live. This seems an appropriate place to ask this question…when you pray, do you believe God hears you and that He will answer your prayers? To know deep in your heart that God hears your prayers and will answer you is what faith is all about. Again, faith is built when we have to go through the tough stuff. James 1:2–4 (NKJV) says it this way, "My brethren, count it all joy when you fall into various trials, knowing that the testing of your faith produces patience. But let patience have its perfect work, that you may be perfect and complete, lacking nothing." Think about that for a moment—isn't this a place where you want to be? Lacking nothing! To get to this kind of faith, we are going to have to go through some things we would rather not have to face at all. When you have that beautiful baby and they are rushed to the NICU, this is where your faith is built!

According to the Strong's Concordance, there are 245 verses in the Bible on "faith." The Passion Translation describes faith this way… "Now faith brings our hopes into reality and becomes the foundation needed to acquire the things we long for. It is all the evidence required to prove what is still unseen" (Hebrews 11:1). Hebrews chapter 11 is the faith chapter in the Bible. This chapter provides many examples of faith, but one of my favorites is the story of Abraham. Let's set the background here…Abraham and Sarah were told by God that they would have a son and that he would be the father of many nations.

Unfortunately, this wasn't something that happened right away. In fact, Abraham and Sarah didn't have Isaac until they were close to one hundred years old. That's a long time to wait to conceive. So it's natural to understand how they could be very protective over Isaac. I'm sure they watched his every move like a helicopter parent. But then God asked Abraham to do something crazy. God asked Abraham to offer up Isaac as a firstborn sacrifice. Abraham didn't question God, not even for a moment. He knew that God had made a promise through his son Isaac, which the Lord had told him in advance, even though Sarah was thought to be barren. He believed with his whole heart that God Himself would provide the sacrifice required. To top all this off, Isaac wasn't a little baby when God asked Abraham to offer Isaac as a sacrifice. He was old enough to make the journey to the place of the sacrifice and old enough to carry the wood for the sacrifice and big enough to climb up on the altar.

In fact, all the examples and stories of great faith mentioned in Hebrews 11 are men and women who endured some especially horrific trials knowing that God would take care of them and lead them through the storm. We are defined by how we are able to persevere through trials. So back to the question about how you pray…do you pray pleading with God, begging Him for a certain outcome? Or do you have faith to believe in God to provide His will in your situation and that His will is ultimately good? Faith never makes you weak; it can only make you stronger. There will be times when your faith will be stronger than anyone else around you. This is where you have to hold to your faith and trust God. When things in the natural look the worst is when God goes to work for you. He is not slack concerning His promises. If God says it, count it done. It won't look the way you think it should look, and it will never be in your time. But God will deliver on His promises. His word will not return void. Isaiah 55:10–12 (NLT) puts it like this:

> The rain and snow come down from the heavens and stay on the ground to water the earth.
> They cause the grain to grow, producing seed for the farmer and bread for the hungry. It
> is the same with my word. I send it out, and it always produces fruit. It will accomplish all
> I want it to, and it will prosper everywhere I send it. You will live in joy and peace. The
> mountains and hills will burst into song, and the trees of the field will clap their hands!

Do you have the kind of faith that can move mountains?

Jesus, I want faith that moves mountains. I need more of You and less of me. Help me empty myself of me and fill me with Your love. I need Your love. In Jesus' name. Amen.

DAY 70:

"He Is Always with Us"

"Let your conduct be without covetousness; be content with such things as you have. For He Himself has said, 'I will never leave you nor forsake you.' So we may boldly say: 'The Lord is my helper; I will not fear. What can man do to me?'"

Hebrews 13:5–6 (NKJV)

Obedience is the key to walking with Jesus. Oh, sweet friends, this can be a very difficult task, but I promise you on the other side of the obedience is a great reward. We must learn to trust Him and just let our faith blossom in His presence. He will *not* let you down…He never has, and He never will.

God's promise that "I will never leave you nor forsake you" is found in multiple books of the Bible, in both the Old and New Testaments. With this promise, we can be assured that He is always with us. This promise should encourage us to stay in alignment with God in faith and spirit. No matter our past, we can always repent and return to God's loving mercy and grace. Let us give thanks for God's glorious love and compassion for us.[18]

You may be going through the most difficult storm in your life. But the promise still stands. We lose sight of Him during these times, and we often look to other sources of comfort. All we have to do is look for Him in every situation. The Bible not only tells us that He will never leave us, but it also says in the second half of Hebrews 13:5–6 that the Lord is our helper. Not only is He never going to leave you, but He is also going to help you through this trial. In this verse He is saying that He is going to come to your aid when you are in distress. Ahhh, the promise gets even richer!

Psalm 118:7–8 (TPT) describes His help this way: "For you stand beside me as my hero who rescues me. I've seen with my own eyes the defeat of my enemies. I've triumphed over them all! Lord, it is so much better to trust in you to save me than to put my confidence in someone else." Nobody can help you in your situation like the Lord. Whether your problems are large or small, His Word stands as the absolute truth.

The catch is we have to seek Him. He is not going to invade our world and take over our lives. That's not in alignment with the word He spoke over Adam where He gave Adam dominion over all the earth. Because Adam sinned and failed to keep his end of the bargain, we are left in a fallen world to

---

18 The BibleStudyTools Staff, comps., "I Will Never Leave You nor Forsake You," posted July 21, 2021, https://www.biblestudytools.com/topical-verses/i-will-never-leave-you-nor-forsake-you/.

fend for ourselves…unless we seek Him with everything. We must seek Him with our entire spirit, soul, and body. Once we seek Him out and express our need to Him, that is when we can expect God to step into the situation. Instead of running to other lovers, seek out the lover of your soul. He's waiting for you. Run to Him.

I am reminded in the Scriptures in 1 Kings 8:57 (NKJV), "May the Lord our God be with us as he was with our fathers. May he never leave us nor forsake us." This is a beautiful promise that we should all grab hold of. My prayer for you today is no matter how hard the road has been for you, you will listen to that still, small voice of the Savior and be obedient in whatever He is calling you to do… Will you do it? What do you have to lose, my friends?

Jesus, thank You for being my trusted friend whom I can run to in times of trouble. Come, Lord Jesus, I need You now. Heal me, and I will be healed. In Jesus' name. Amen.

DAY 71:

"Look to Heaven"

"Since you have been raised to new life with Christ, set your sights on the realities of heaven, where Christ sits in the place of honor at God's right hand. Think about the things of heaven, not the things of earth."

Colossians 3:1–2 (NLT)

As I was reading Psalm 27, I was reminded that King David was a man after God's own heart! He was a worshiper and not a worrier! He knew God on an intimate level, so he would praise and worship his way through all stages in life, the good and the bad. David had everything a man could want in life. He had wealth, power, authority, respect, and adoration. He faced many enemies and battles throughout his life, but he always knew where his help came from! You see, to experience spiritual intimacy with Jesus, you must seek Him! Jeremiah 29:13 (NKJV) urges us that if "you will seek Me and find Me, when you search for Me with all your heart."

In times of trying circumstances, we can decide between two choices. We can either try to figure a way through the circumstances out of our flesh or turn our eyes to heaven, where our true help comes from. It's only natural for us to turn toward the flesh because we tend to easily worry about the circumstances surrounding our life. It's all too close to us, and sometimes we can't see the forest for all the trees. But what we should be looking for is divine understanding and strategy. The kind of help that comes from above is from the Lord who made heaven and earth. (See Psalm 121:1–2.) There is no place for help like the Word of God. The Word has answers for every situation. All God's healing work begins with His Word. The problem with help that comes from our flesh is that it is subjective at best. Because we are too close to the situation, we seldom can see the situation from a higher perspective. This is exactly why we need to seek God.

You may be in a place where you have no idea where to turn, let alone how to get to a place of peace. But when we turn to God and His Word, we can suddenly obtain answers to the problems we are facing. The Word of God is living and active. Though the Word never changes, you could read the same passage every day and get something different out of it each day. There are so many treasures in the Bible just waiting to be discovered. It's also how we learn about the character and nature of God Himself. This is just one of the many reasons we should be reading the Word of God daily; in doing so, we will find the heart of God.

Losing a baby can feel like a wilderness season in life. It's like somebody dropped us off in the middle of the Sahara Desert with no directions or any idea how to get out of the desert. The heat is intensified. The atmosphere is dry and barren. And the loneliness is unbearable. You can be surrounded by people yet feel completely alone. The good thing about the wilderness seasons of our life is that they cause us to rely upon God wholly and completely. The apostle Paul struggled with a thorn in his flesh, and he pleaded with the Lord to remove it. But the Lord responded to Paul's plea in 2 Corinthians 12:8 (NKJV), "My grace is sufficient for you, for My strength is made perfect in weakness." Therefore, most gladly I will rather boast in my infirmities that the power of Christ may rest upon me. Paul was essentially saying thank goodness for my weakness because I sure need Your strength, Lord.

You may be struggling and in a lot of pain right now. I encourage you to rest in Christ; He is refining you and making you stronger. The love of Christ is amazing and will cushion you through the rough spots in life. But you must stay grounded in Him. It's our responsibility to seek Him and to draw near to Him. When we draw near to Him, He will draw near to us. Look at these scriptures in Psalm 56 and tell me God doesn't care about your pain:

> *You've kept track of all my wandering and my weeping. You've stored my many tears in your bottle—not one will be lost. For they are all recorded in your book of remembrance. The very moment I call to you for a father's help the tide of battle turns, and my enemies flee. This one thing I know: God is on my side! I trust in the Lord. And I praise him! I trust in the Word of God. And I praise him! What harm could man do to me? With God on my side, I will not be afraid of what comes. My heart overflows with praise to God and for his promises. I will always trust in him.*

Psalm 56:8–11 (TPT)

God is keeping records of your pain and every tear you've cried. He has written a book of remembrance about you. God sees you and He takes notice when you are in pain. Take your pain and look to heaven from where your help comes from. Are you ready to surrender your pain to God and rest in His love?

Jesus, my pain is so real right now. Please come into this and let me feel Your love and healing over my situation. I need You, Lord. In Jesus' name. Amen.

DAY 72:

"Dare to Hope"

"I will never forget this awful time, as I grieve over my loss. Yet I still dare to hope when I remember this: The faithful love of the Lord never ends! His mercies never cease. Great is his faithfulness; his mercies begin afresh each morning."

Lamentations 3:20–23 (NLT)

Today is Memorial Day as I sit down to write. This is a day to remember all our fallen heroes who have fought so valiantly for our country and gave their all. Parents have lost sons or daughters, and wives have lost their husbands. This is a day to remember the sacrifices these men and women have made for our country. These are true patriots, and today we salute you!

But I am also reminded of when a soldier is stationed abroad or a sailor is out to sea. Imagine a young soldier who had only shortly married his bride when he was deployed in a foreign battleground. There was such hope and optimism in his life and in his marriage, the excitement of family planning and deciding where they wanted to plant roots. Shortly before the soldier deploys for his mission, the young couple finds out they are pregnant with their first child. The excitement builds even more for this family as the husband embarks on a journey…he will go from a young boy and return a man, a husband, and a father.

Months later he receives word that his wife is ready to go into labor. By the grace of God, he is able to receive leave and go home for the birth of his child. The young soldier enters the hospital and enquires about his bride and newborn baby. He enters the labor and delivery room and hears all kinds of commotion. Something doesn't seem right! Although he has never experienced the birth of a child before, there is an inner knowing that tells him something is wrong. His parents greet him near the door with excitement to see him, but they have a sense of dread on their face. His dad tells him, "Son, there's a problem with the birth, and both your wife and your baby are in jeopardy." He goes on to say, "You will have a son if he survives." The soldier drops the flowers he stopped to get for his wife and begins asking question after question. Suddenly, the doctor comes out of the room looking exhausted; he says the young soldier's name and takes him away to a private room. The doctor proceeds to tell him they did all they could to save his wife and child, but there was nothing else that could be done. Both his wife and child died during birth. The hope and excitement that he so eagerly entered the hospital leave him, and he is left with nothing but pain and anguish!

In this case, this is a fictional story, but these kinds of stories happen every day in real life. How would you feel if you were placed in this young soldier's combat boots? You would be faced with going back to your mission having lost your first child and your wife on the same day. Would you have any hope? Would you be able to effectively do the job that you have been trained to do? Would you still feel like a well-oiled fighting machine? My guess is this would be the most difficult battle of your life!

This is a time and place in your life where you would find yourself at a crossroads. You must choose to find hope wherever you can and be brave enough to be able to find expectation again. People find themselves in storms like this every day. You must choose to live life and love again when these storms hit. This is where we surrender our hopes and dreams to the Father and give Him full access to our whole life, to our hopes and our dreams. This is where we must trust Him with everything!

Get a heart full of expectation again! Expect to see Jesus in everyday life. Have the courage to have expectations again in your life. I am reminded of all the miracles Jesus did throughout his life and how we can still see these miracles today. Imagine being this soldier and seeing himself getting married again, seeing the miracle of looking into the eyes of his first newborn baby while remembering the loss of life that could have been. That's Jesus calling you deeper into His love. Jesus is calling you today. He is beckoning you to come deeper into His love, into a place of deep intimacy with Him. This is the place where expectation is birthed. Call upon Him, friends, and seek Him where He can be found. The Bible says we have not because we ask not (see James 4:2). I encourage you in this new season of life to call out to Him and ask for His help wherever you may need it. Invite Him into that very place of need, whether it be a place of healing, a financial need, or some other miracle that is needed. Invite Him into that place. Seek His face and not His hand. He will be there for you…He is waiting with nail-scarred hands, saying, "Come to Me." Friends, go ahead and run into His open arms. What are you waiting for?

Jesus, I need Your help today. I am giving You all my pain and grief, and I am believing You will help me walk through this difficult season in my life. I need Your love to wash over me right here and right now. In Jesus' name. Amen.

DAY 73:

"Comforted By God"

"Blessed be the God and Father of our Lord Jesus Christ, the Father of mercies and God of all comfort, who comforts us in all our tribulation, that we may be able to comfort those who are in any trouble, with the comfort with which we ourselves are comforted by God."

2 Corinthians 1:3–4 (NKJV)

The following story is from a treasured supporter of Angels in Waiting 91:4. Her story was shared with us on our Testimony Thursday for our social media sites. This is Erik's story:

"Two years ago, on June 15th, 2021, our son Erik was born at twenty-seven point three weeks. My water broke at eighteen point five weeks, and I was miraculously admitted to Labor and Delivery. The doctor came in, grave-faced, and told my husband and me there were two options for our situation—probably deliver a baby who may or may not be alive in the next twenty-four to forty-eight hours or have an abortion. We told the doctor abortion was not an option for us and we would 'ride this bus as far as it went.' We told him we were people of prayer who were believing God for a miracle for our son. He nodded and said he hoped the best of us.

"Against all odds, through the miraculous strength of God, I carried Erik to twenty-seven weeks, three days. He was born breathing on his own (another miracle) and moved his little arm! The doctors and medical staff were amazed. We had no doubt our son would be the miracle baby talked about for years, as he would grow into an amazing adult and change the world.

"People around the world were praying for Erik. People we didn't know would message us and tell us their Bible study in Canada, their church in the UK, their home group in Israel were praying for Erik. We were overwhelmed and so, *so* grateful! We never doubted our son would come home alive. Even his medical team were planning for his homecoming day. We would walk into his tiny NICU (neonatal intensive care unit) room, and the nurses would say, 'Your baby is so present; we never see that with NICU babies.'

"On September 2nd, at 8:30 a.m., we got a call that shattered our world forever; Erik had died. 'No, *no, no*!' my mind screamed! My husband and I rushed to the hospital; our favorite nurse rocking his lifeless body; our doctor coming in and telling us he did not see it going this way; even our doctor's mom had been praying for Erik. There is not an adequate word in the English language to describe the anguish

175

in that moment of the death of our son.

"I have always had a very close relationship with Jesus, but in this time of pain, I found myself so angry that I couldn't speak to Him! The flood of *why* was relentless! One day I could feel the Lord's presence near; I just knew He was going to drop the hammer and scold me for being so angry and not talking to Him.

"'What?' I angrily said in my heart. 'What do *You* want!' The Lord quietly whispered to my heart, 'Kerrie, I'm patient with grief. You take all the time you need.' Those words broke open a dam of tears, and I was overcome by the love of Jesus in a way I didn't know existed! I began to ask Him, 'Why?'

"I remember a person I respected saying after losing their father, 'If you can get past the *why*, you will move into a realm of intimacy with God you didn't know existed.' I wanted my heart to just 'get there,' but that *why* question was so unresolved that it was becoming a constant battle to not have an answer. One day I was wrestling with the *why* question *again*, and I said, 'Why, God! *Why did You take my son*!'

"And the quiet reply to my heart was, 'What if he chose?' What? Chose? Erik chose to go to heaven? *This* was an entirely new perspective! I told my husband, and he said, 'Kerrie, if Erik chose to go to heaven, we can't hold that against him.'

"About nine months later, a close friend was visiting with her family; they had prayed with us for Erik and had fasted for Erik and our family when we weren't able to because of pumping etc. It meant more than I can say! One day we were talking, and I told her what I felt like the Lord had said to my heart. She said, 'Did I ever tell you about what the Lord told me after Erik died?' I shook my head no. My friend then went on to tell me that after Erik had died, she mourned as if she'd lost a nephew (we are very close friends), and she asked the Lord, 'Was it me? Did we not pray enough? Could we have done more?'

"The Lord showed her a picture of Him showing Erik two pictures: the first was he was a healthy kid who would grow up in a happy, loving home; the second picture was if Erik went to heaven (died), his life would impact many people for God's kingdom! I was stunned and overwhelmed and so proud of my son and so amazed at God's faithfulness, even in the midst of such pain and heartache!

"No two stories are the same; mommas aren't supposed to lose babies! But the thing I am learning in such a powerful way is the gift God has given us in free choice! He never forces us to do something; He lovingly leads us. He only wants good for us; this very broken world is the cause of sin and evil and chaos and pain. We can choose our own way, or we can choose to follow the path of the Lord and the life it brings, even when there's sorrow or pain.

"Ephesians 6:12 (ESV), 'For we do not wrestle against flesh and blood, but against the rulers, against the authorities, against the cosmic powers over this present darkness, against the spiritual forces of evil in the heavenly places.'

"Please know, in your grief, you are seen, and you are so loved by your Creator and Father God. Humanity was never designed for death; that came out of a broken relationship with God; it's also why it's so heavy. If I could wrap my arms around you and give you the biggest, longest hug, I would! I am so sorry you have lost a child; it's not fair; it's not okay; it's not right; it's the awful outcome of a very broken world, but please know the Spirit of Truth loves you beyond anything else and wants you to know His love and truth in the most real way possible.

"There are so many, many things I have learned from my young son's life, even as I miss him daily and grieve him often. I am learning not to waste our free choice on anything other than the Spirit of Truth and living from that truth and that love, which is only found in Jesus."

Erik's mom

As Christians, we often quote Romans 8:28 (NKJV), which, in short, says, "All things work together for good for those who love the Lord." As Christians we often quote this verse when something has not quite gone right in our lives in hopes that God will somehow turn it all around for us. We want to believe this verse so much, but there is often part of us, especially during great times of loss, such as losing a child, that can't see how any good can come of it. But Erik's story shows that sometimes our children may have more impact in their death than they could if they had lived a full life. And that our babies may just have a choice in the matter. I've heard of many other near-death experiences where people were offered a choice to experience all that heaven has to offer or come back to earth to live out our God-given purpose. There really is no wrong choice in these situations. Let's not forget our loved ones sometimes have a choice to return and live out a good life or stay in heaven and impact more lives for Christ than we could ever hope to imagine. We don't often get to know if there was a choice to be made. One thing is for certain…our children are a blessing from the Lord. Did you catch that word? *From.* It says in Jeremiah 1:5 (GNT), "I chose you before I gave you life, and before you were born I selected you." So, as our children pass from this life to heaven, they truly are going home to be with their true Father. The draw of returning to Papa God is sometimes too strong for our sweet babies to overcome, as much as they love their earthly parents too. Would you come back if you were given a choice?

Jesus, I am so grateful for You and for heaven. Help me in this time of grief to come to You and just be still in Your presence. Lord, heal me of any unbelief I may be carrying as I walk through this season of my life. In Jesus' mighty name. Amen.

DAY 74:

"Blessed Assurance"

" 'You have nothing to fear. I will take care of you and your children.' So he reassured them with kind words that touched their hearts."

Genesis 50:21 (GNT)

Friends, many have experienced the loss of babies and were afraid to try to get pregnant again. Disappointment and fear paralyze us from moving forward with the plan that God has for us. Many have prayed and prayed for a child only to be disappointed time and again. But God wants you to persevere through the disappointment and fear to keep moving toward His promises to you. Do you know the promises that God has made to you? His Word is full of promises to His people. But we can also receive promises through revelation knowledge.

When it comes to experiencing loss and still holding onto faith and the promises of God, nobody did it better than Job. Job was a righteous man who was blameless and upright in all he did. He shunned evil and feared God. Job was a wealthy man and had a loving family. Job even offered sacrifices on behalf of his children just in case they had sinned and cursed God in their hearts (Job 1:5).

One day Satan came before God, and God asked him if he had considered his servant Job. Satan told God that Job had everything he ever needed or wanted because God had protected him and provided for his needs. Satan went on to tell God, "I bet if You touched all that he had, then he would surely curse You." God said, "Okay…all that Job has is in your power—only don't touch his body." Next, Job had a messenger come up to him and told Job that his children's oxen and donkeys were carried off by enemies and the servants were killed by the sword. No one was left except for the messenger. While that messenger was still speaking, another messenger came and told him that the fire of God fell from heaven and burned up the sheep and his servants. Another messenger came and told him all his camels had been stolen. Then yet another came and told him all his children were at his oldest son's house having a party when a great wind came across the wilderness and struck the four corners of the house, and it fell on the young people, and they were all dead. Job got up quickly, tore his robe, and shaved his head and fell to the ground and worshipped. In Job 1:21 (NKJV), "And he said: 'Naked I came from my mother's womb, And naked shall I return there. The Lord gave, and the Lord has taken away; Blessed be the name of the Lord.'"

I don't know about you, but I'm not sure that worshipping God would be my first response after all that had happened to Job. But this demonstrates Job's impeccable character. But in Job 2 the story continues in much the same way as it began. Again, God asks Satan if he has considered his servant Job even after Satan had incited God against him to destroy him without cause. Satan said something to the effect that a man will give up everything he has to save his own life, but if you take away his health, then he will surely curse God. God said, "All right, do with him as you please, but spare his life." So Satan struck Job's body with painful boils from head to foot. It was so bad that Job's wife came to him and said, "Are you still trying to maintain your integrity? Curse God and die." Job told her, "Should we only accept good things from God and never anything bad?" Job said or did nothing wrong. Even Job's friends tried to tell him that he had to have sinned against God. Job suffered greatly losing all he had and all his family.

As we fast forward to the end of the book of Job in chapter 42 after Job had persevered through the greatest storm in life, Job repents for any doubt that he had or blame that he had put on God. God rewarded Job with double his possessions and seven more sons and three more daughters. His daughters were more beautiful than any other women in all the land and Job gave them an inheritance among their brothers. Giving an inheritance to daughters in this time and culture was simply not done prior to Job. Not only did God doubly bless Job, but He also allowed Job to live for another one hundred and forty years.

Have you ever felt like Job? Maybe you have lost everything too like Job. Maybe you have lost hope in ever having a family. Can you reach down deep within yourself to honor God while you are still enduring the hardships? Hold fast and look to the goodness of God. Even when life has taken everything from you, if you can just hold onto Him and never let go, God will bless your faithfulness. God has planned our lives out from the beginning; He even knows when we are going to choose a different path than the path He has planned for us. God will make a way where there seems to be no way. But we have to hold onto our faith in God and trust Him in all His ways. Just like with Job, God believes in us and knows that we are capable of standing firm in the face of great adversity. Sometimes all you have to do is…*stand*! My advice to you is the same advice the apostle Peter had in 1 Peter 5:6–10 (NKJV):

> *Therefore humble yourselves under the mighty hand of God, that He may exalt you in due time, casting all your care upon Him, for He cares for you. Be sober, be vigilant; because your adversary the devil walks about like a roaring lion, seeking whom he may devour. Resist him, steadfast in the faith, knowing that the same sufferings are experienced by your brotherhood in the world. But may the God of all grace, who called us to His eternal glory by Christ Jesus, after you have suffered a while, perfect, establish, strengthen, and settle you.*

Do you trust God in the middle of great trials?

Jesus, forgive me for any unbelief I may have in me and help me to listen to Your voice and keep my eyes on You. In Jesus' name. Amen.

DAY 75:

"Serpent"

"Now the serpent was more cunning than any beast of the field which the Lord God had made. And he said to the woman, 'Has God indeed said, "You shall not eat of every tree of the garden"?'"

Genesis 3:1 (NKJV)

I saw a video recently, and a large snake was at the veterinarian's office, stretched across the examination table. The doctor was pulling out an object, which was a golf club. I couldn't believe my eyes. I stared at the video as she pulled out something else, and to my amazement it was the owner's clothing. I saw the owner of the snake say, "Oh, thank goodness my snake will be okay now," as she showed so much joy. I thought about it for a little bit, and God spoke to me so loudly about this…"He" said, "Why do you think this snake ate these items?" I was dumbfounded…"I truly don't know." "He" let me know a snake is a snake…it was sizing up its owner to eat her! As she stood there so happy her snake had been saved, the snake did *not* feel the same about her. That takes me to Paul in Acts 28:3–5 (NIV):

Paul gathered a pile of brushwood and, as he put it on the fire, a viper, driven out by the heat, fastened itself on his hand. When the islanders saw the snake hanging from his hand, they said to each other, "This man must be a murderer; for though he escaped from the sea, the goddess Justice has not allowed him to live." But Paul shook the snake off into the fire and suffered no ill effects.

That, my friends, is a powerful verse! Paul suffered *no* ill effects! Wow, that's the God we serve! "He" watches out for us when we are in the fire! You see, a snake is a snake no matter what we try to do for it. It was cursed from the beginning.

So the Lord God said to the serpent, "Because you have done this, You are cursed more than all cattle, And more than every beast of the field; On your belly you shall go, and you shall eat dust all the days of your life" (Genesis 3:14, NKJV).

You see, the snake was cunning and always hiding in the dark, looking for a way to strike.

"Now the serpent was more cunning than any beast of the field that the Lord God had made. And he said to the woman, 'Has God indeed said, "You shall not eat of every tree of the garden"?'" (Genesis 3:1, NKJV).

Much like the devil…he waits for the perfect time to strike, but we have so much hope in Jesus because "He" has given us the authority through "His" shed blood to stomp on the enemy!

"Behold, I give you the authority to trample on serpents and scorpions, and over all the power of the enemy, and nothing shall by any means hurt you" (Luke 10:19, NKJV). God has equipped us with the authority of the name of Jesus; do not allow the enemy to blind your mind from that right.

That, my friends, should give you so much hope for your future! We must remember who our fight is against: the evil one, Satan!

"For we do not wrestle against flesh and blood, but against principalities, against powers, against the rulers of the darkness of this age, against spiritual hosts of wickedness in the heavenly places" (Ephesians 6:12, NKJV).

It reminds me of the verse in Revelation 12:9 (NKJV), "So the great dragon was cast out, that serpent of old, called the Devil and Satan, who deceives the whole world; he was cast to the earth, and his angels were cast out with him." So with all this in mind I will leave you with this…what serpent in your life is sizing you up?

Jesus, keep me safe from the enemy. Help me to hear Your voice and obey. Send Your angels to guard and protect my family and me. In Jesus' mighty name. Amen.

DAY 76:

"Light of Eternity"

We view our slight, short-lived troubles in the light of eternity. We see our difficulties as the substance that produces for us an eternal, weighty glory far beyond all comparison, because we don't focus our attention on what is seen but on what is unseen. For what is seen is temporary, but the unseen realm is eternal.

2 Corinthians 4:17–18 (TPT)

This may seem like a difficult time in your life right now, but at the end of your story is a light that far outweighs the troubles you are going through. There is always purpose for your pain. You will eventually see how God will take your pain and see how God will turn it for His glory. There is redemption, there is hope, and there is healing. God doesn't cause this pain. But He will turn the enemy's plan around for your good and His glory. I am reminded of Romans 8:28 (NKJV), "And we know that all things work together for good to those who love God, to those who are the called according to His purpose." It doesn't say He will work a few things out for us or even most things; it says He works *all* things together for good. The caveat is that you must love God and be called according to His purpose. But guess what? If you have accepted Jesus Christ as your Savior, then you have been called.

You may not see it now, but it is clear from 2 Corinthians 4 that our difficulties are producing for us an eternal, weighty glory. We should keep in mind the last part of this scripture—what we see now is only temporary. It's a season in our life. When we bear down and walk out our salvation, even in the most difficult of times, we are putting our focus on the unseen realm, which is eternal. When we are experiencing something, such as the death of a child, we often cannot see past the moment we are in. It is difficult to look past our present circumstances to see the glory that is yet to be revealed. It's in these moments, however, when God grows us up and matures us in our faith. We must be stretched in order to grow. It is painful; make no mistake about it. This is where we must put all our trust and faith in God that He really will work it out for our good.

I especially like the first part of today's scripture, which basically says in light of eternity our troubles are very short-lived. Think of it in these terms…seventy or eighty years in light of eternity is but a moment. Often the storms we go through are much shorter than that. Your perspective on your troubles will determine how you overcome them. If you view your troubles as momentary, then you will be able to get on the other side much faster than if you view them as a lifetime of hurt and pain. Think about

Job—he lost everything he had worked so hard for, all the things that God had blessed his life with. Even though he initially felt sorry for himself, he looked in the mirror and decided to put his faith in God. "If He did it for me once, He would surely do it for me again…" must have been his mentality.

Job saw His troubles as momentary. He kept his eye on the Father and placed all His trust in Him. I'm certain Job didn't forget about his family that he lost, but God rewarded Job double for his trouble. Why? Because Job put His trust in the Father above, not in the things of this earth. Job remained faithful even amid great tragedy in his life.

There's an old hymn called "Turn Your Eyes Upon Jesus" with lyrics that go like this, "Turn you eyes upon Jesus, look full into His wonderful face, and the things of earth will grow strangely dim in the light of His glory and grace."

How about you? Are you looking to Jesus? Can you say you maintained your faith through the storm you are going through?

Jesus, help me walk through this very difficult time in my life and get the healing I need from You. I want to keep my eyes on You. I need You, Jesus. Amen.

DAY 77:

"Love Is the Prize"

"Until then, there are three things that remain: faith, hope, and love—yet love surpasses them all. So above all else, let love be the beautiful prize for which you run."

1 Corinthians 13:13 (TPT)

Imagine being a grandmother knowing that your grandchild would be stillborn. This is the story of another one of our founding volunteers. She is a retired neonatal intensive care unit (NICU) nurse. So this was not something new to her. But now she had to come up close and personal with the pain of having a stillborn. This is the story of her son, daughter-in-law, and granddaughter, Hazel Rose.

"Hazel, you were to be my sixth grandchild. The baby when we thought there would be no more. We were all so excited for a new life, pink bows and pigtails, little girl giggles. I was retiring after forty-two years of nursing and twenty-two years working in the NICU.

"Over the years I have been with many families when they received the news that 'there is nothing more we can do.' I have held moms and dads, prayed with them, bathed the newborn, and so tenderly dressed their precious baby before they held them for the last time. I have cried and laughed with many families through tragedy and triumph. I have sent happy babies home with loving parents, and I have sent babies to foster homes. I have had many nights of lost sleep wondering what would become of those sent to foster homes, or are the critical ones improving, and how are the parents holding up? These were just a few of the things that ran through my mind almost on a daily basis.

"I've seen a lot. As a healthcare provider, you have to separate yourself from the situation as best you can, but it's not easily done. I have come home and wept for the loss, shattered dreams, and heartache I knew was to come for families. But none of this prepared me for losing my granddaughter. When I got the call, I had to go immediately to be with my son and daughter-in-law. During a routine ultrasound, no heartbeat was detected at seventeen weeks. Where was God? How could this happen? I caught the earliest flight I could find to lend support to my family.

"When I was checking in at the airport, the gentleman called for a wheelchair, even though I hadn't asked for one. You see, I had broken my foot and was in a walking boot. I hadn't even thought about how hard the Atlanta airport would be to navigate in a boot. Fortunately, a sweet young man came to my rescue. I told him where I was going, and we began to talk as he guided me through the airport. He spoke of his wife, and I asked if there were children, and he began to share of their loss about one year prior. I told him why I was traveling, and he said he would pray for my family. There is no coincidence with God and how He works things out.

"I arrived at my destination where my other children would arrive later. We were all there for support. Hazel's birth took several long, sad, and grueling days. I'm no different than any other mother; when your kids hurt, your heart is broken. Our hearts were being shattered at the prospect of losing a baby. We wrapped Hazel in preparation for her journey to heaven, and we spoke her name into the atmosphere and told her how beautiful she was. She was fragile and tiny and oh so loved. She was held by all of us, and we said our goodbyes. The chaplain came in and wanted to share a poem with us she had just been introduced to a few days before…"

> And in this he showed me a little thing, the quantity of a hazel nut, lying in the palm of my hand, as it seemed. And it was as round as any ball. I looked upon it with the eye of my understanding, and thought, "What may this be?" And it was answered generally thus, 'It is all that is made." I marveled how it might last, for I thought it might suddenly have fallen to nothing for littleness. And I was answered in my understanding: It lasts and ever shall, for God loves it. And so have all things their beginning by the love of God. In this little thing I saw three properties. The first is that God made it. The second that God loves it. And the third, that God keeps it.
>
> **Julian of Norwich,** *Revelations of Divine Love*

As our volunteer returned home, we came together as a group and bought her a lemon tree. A lemon tree is a sign of hope. I had been praying about what to do for her and her family, and God clearly spoke about how the lemon tree is a sign of hope. So we bought the tree and gave it to her. As we gave this gift, we read the poem that was given to her family and made the connection that the hazel nut was mentioned. We gave her a lemon tree as a gift (who does that?), and she would remember her Hazel Rose every time she would see this tree. Oddly enough, that little lemon tree produced fruit the first year she received it. Lemon trees do not usually produce fruit for a couple of years. This was God's gift to this family. It was as if He was saying, "I see your pain, but remember there is always hope in Me." Sometimes you just have to grab onto the little things, any little thing that produces hope in you.

I was reminded of 1 Peter 1:3 (TPT), which says, "Celebrate with praises the God and Father of our Lord Jesus Christ, who has shown us his extravagant mercy. For his fountain of mercy has given us a new life—we are reborn to experience a living, energetic hope through the resurrection of Jesus Christ from the dead." Jesus is our ultimate hope! For Hazel Rose, she is experiencing the joy of heaven every single day. She never for a moment was faced with the wickedness of this world. She never endured sadness or depression or even encountered mean people. Her last breath inside her mother's womb was her first breath in the kingdom of God. Can you just imagine the joy she must have felt?

So, if you are enduring the pain of this kind of loss as a mother, a grandmother, or whatever, just know that while we mourn here on this earth, there is a celebration in heaven for the one who has gone home to be with their Savior. Are you able to find hope in the midst of loss?

Jesus, help me find hope in the middle of my loss. Come heal all these places that feel so raw and walk with me through the storm. I need You. In Jesus' mighty name. Amen.

DAY 78:

"Cry Out to the Lord"

"But in my distress I cried out to the Lord; yes, I prayed to my God for help. He heard me from his sanctuary; my cry to him reached his ears."

Psalm 18:6 (NLT)

Do you cry out to God when you are in distress? That's an interesting question, isn't it? Our God is not deaf. He does hear us, and He will not turn away from us when we cry out to Him, seeking comfort and relief. He sees our tears, shares our grief, understands our sorrows, and hears our cries of anguish and suffering. God is well acquainted with our grief. Remember God gave up His one and only Son by sending Him from His divine position to the earth to take on human flesh. Jesus lived on earth fully human for thirty-three years. When it came time for Jesus to fulfill His mission, the Father wept just like an earthly father weeps over losing his child. Yes…the Father knew the plan from the beginning, and He knew it would take a perfect, spotless/sinless sacrifice to fulfill the requirements of the law. The only one capable of making this sacrifice was Jesus.

You might be thinking, *That's all well and good, but the Father knew His Son would be resurrected and was returning back home to heaven.* This is very true. But He also knows your future, too, but he doesn't take away your free will because of poor choices or bad decisions that you might make. You are not alone in your loss. Bad things happen to good people every single day. We can't shelter our lives from the business of living; otherwise, we will never leave the house.

Adam and Eve conceived and had two sons, Cain and Abel. You probably know the story about these two brothers. Cain was a farmer, and his brother, Abel, was a skilled shepherd who took care of the family's animals. The boys made sacrifices to God, but God favored Abel's sacrifice instead of Cain's. Cain brought some of produce of the land, while Abel brought the firstborn of his sheep. God favored Abel's sacrifice because it was an offering from the best Abel had to give. This made Cain very angry and jealous. Cain then plotted a plan to kill his brother, Abel, out in the field with a rock. The Lord called out to Cain to inquire about his brother, Abel, but Cain lied to God. God punished Cain pretty severely, as he was no longer able to grow crops on his land. However, God kept Cain from being murdered, thus sparing his life.

But put yourself in the shoes of Eve, the mother of both boys. Her baby was killed by the oldest child out of a fit of rage and jealousy. Oh, the pain and grief that Eve must have endured. Not only did she lose one son to death, but the other son was as good as dead and became a vagabond. In essence, Eve lost both of her children. How does a mother go on with life after a tragedy like this? What thoughts must have gone through her head? I'm certain Adam experienced many of the same feelings as Eve. But being a mother of sons myself, I can tell you this news must have been completely devastating to Eve. There is a special bond between a mother and a son.

Let's dig a little deeper into this story. Cain and Abel were the first two individuals born with a sinful nature. Since their births occurred after the fall of man by Adam, they were the first two born to two people who had sinned before God. From this point on, every generation would have the same sinful nature as Cain and Abel. Eve rejoiced before the Lord at Cain's birth, saying, "I have acquired a man from the Lord" (Genesis 4:1, NKJV).

> *God promised to redeem humanity from the curse of sin through the male offspring of Eve…*
>
> *By God's design, childbearing is a blessing of marriage. Cain's birth was significant for a couple reasons. First, it was proof of God's faithfulness since He had not withheld His goodness from them, allowing them to bear children despite their sinfulness.[19]*

Second, as a male child, Cain was the first hopeful prospect for God's promised redeemer. It is safe to say that Eve expressed the same exuberance over Abel's birth as she did with Cain. Both represented two opportunities for God to redeem humanity through her offspring. So, when she lost both of her children, one to death and the other to separation, she also lost both of her chances for God to redeem humanity after the sin she and Adam committed. She not only lost her children but also lost her chance at redemption. But God…

> *And Adam knew his wife again, and she bore a son and named him Seth, "For God has appointed another seed for me instead of Abel, whom Cain killed." And as for Seth, to him also a son was born; and he named him Enosh. Then men began to call on the name of the Lord.*

Genesis 4:25–26 (NKJV)

God is not slack in fulfilling His promises. If He said it, He will do it. He is not a man like you or me that He should go back on His word. Maybe you have been given some promises from God. Do you believe what God has said, even though His timing is not your timing?

Jesus, help me trust and believe in Your Word and walk in Your ways. In Jesus' name. Amen.

---

19 Stephen Baker, "Cain and Abel—Bible Story," last updated February 8, 2024, https://www.biblestudytools.com/bible-stories/cain-and-abel.html.

DAY 79:

"Victory"

"The Lord your God in your midst, The Mighty One, will save; He will rejoice over you with gladness, He will quiet you with His love, He will rejoice over you with singing."

Zephaniah 3:17 (NKJV)

Jesus hung on that cross for you and me! He would have died on that cross even if He had to die for just one person...*you.* Can you even wrap your mind around that? He loved *you* enough to die for *you*! "Greater love has no one than this: to lay down one's life for one's friends" (John 15:13, NKJV). Oh, how He loves us even enough to endure the cross! That, my friends, is true love! That's a love I want! I want more of Him and less of me! Seek Him, and you will find Him! "You will seek Me and find Me, when you search for Me with all your heart" (Jeremiah 29:13, NKJV). Seek Him while He may be found. He's waiting on you! What are you waiting on, my friend? Chase after Him! I pray today that you will run after Him and grab hold of the edge of His cloak. "Just then a woman who had been subject to bleeding for twelve years came up behind him and touched the edge of his cloak. She said to herself, 'If I only touch his cloak, I will be healed'" (Matthew 9:21). All it takes is one touch from Him. This is when miracles happen!

The Mighty One, the Maker of Heaven and Earth, loves you with an everlasting love that no love on this earth could ever compare with. In Zechariah 2:8, He calls us the apple of His eye. I think sometimes we overuse this phrase and don't really understand the meaning behind it. The *apple of my eye* is a Hebrew idiom; according to the Jerusalem Prayer Team, it is a phrase translated from the original Hebrew language meaning the most precious and dearest thing one has. For most of us, I think we find it hard to believe that we are the most important thing God has or the most precious thing. Those are bold words! Yet God made a way for all of us to be the "apple of His eye." God gave His one and only Son, Jesus, to be the way for us to become the "apple of His eye." We are the object of His vision and His protection. As a believer in this good, good Father and His Son, Jesus, I know that I have never felt so secure and so loved, even when bad things happen. His love changes things: I know it's changed my heart and has motivated me to please Him more and more. "So shall My word be that goes forth from My mouth; It shall not return to Me void, But it shall accomplish what I please, And it shall prosper in the thing for which I sent it" (Isaiah 55:11, NKJV).

The cross is our ultimate victory. The cross is a blood covenant between the Father and the Son established on our behalf. Jesus was the perfect, spotless lamb…the only suitable sacrifice to cover our sins once and for all. The covenant is not a contract; the covenant is a commitment of love freely given and bound with a sacred oath. This oath established a family bound together with an unbreakable life and death relationship. It was because of this new blood covenant that you and I can be redeemed by His blood. We don't have to do anything to earn it; it is a gift freely given out of His love for us. It is by His grace and His grace alone that we are blood covenant partners and can partake in His lovingkindness today. Jesus is the propitiation of our sins because He gave all for everyone. I would highly recommend you read the book *The Power of the Blood Covenant* by Malcolm Smith. This is an excellent resource and will teach you just what it means to be in a blood covenant with Jesus Christ.

When I hear the word "victory," my mind goes immediately to that old gospel hymn "Victory in Jesus" by E. M. Bartlett. The chorus of this old hymn goes like this:

> O, victory in Jesus, my Savior forever
>
> He sought me and bought me with His redeeming blood
>
> He loved me 'ere I knew Him and all my love is due Him
>
> He plunged me to victory beneath the cleansing flood

Jesus is your victory over everything that life can throw at you, even your own sins. Jesus loved us with a love that we can't fully comprehend until one day we arrive in heaven to be with Him. His love and His blood covenant are the greatest gifts we have ever known, and there is nothing this side of heaven that can compare with His unfailing love.

> *When I saw him, I fell down at his feet as good as dead, but he laid his right hand on me and I heard his reassuring voice saying: Don't yield to fear. I am the Beginning and I am the End, the Living One! I was dead, but now look—I am alive forever and ever. And I hold the keys that unlock death and the unseen world.*

Revelation 1:17–18 (TPT)

The only question I have for you is…are you living in victory?

> *Jesus, I know there is victory in Your blood and in Your Word. Help me lean on You in times of trouble and trust in Your Word! Cover me in Your precious blood and protect me from all evil. In Jesus' name. Amen.*

DAY 80:

"Let Joy Be Your Guide"

"A merry heart does good, like medicine, But a broken spirit dries the bones."

Proverbs 17:22 (NKJV)

John 15:11 (NKJV) says, "These things I have spoken to you, that My joy may remain in you, and that your joy may be full." As I read that verse, I am reminded that my joy can only come from Him! When was the last time you had a good ole belly laugh? You know the kind, the kind of laughter where it brings tears to your eyes and you have trouble catching your breath. How did that laughter make you feel? I bet you were not worried about many things, sad, depressed, or thinking on things of a negative nature. I would bet that you were full of joy. When this kind of joy suddenly hits you, everything in the world fades away…if even for a moment. Laughter really is good medicine. Now think about the worst times of your life when the sadness was so overwhelming that you couldn't even think straight. Every tiny problem is like it's put under a microscope…it becomes so blown out of proportion that making a sensible decision seems impossible. Look at these two extremes and notice how you are feeling by even talking about it. One of the extremes brings joy and happy memories, while the other extreme causes you to think on something extremely sad, maybe even debilitating.

I think at this point it's important to note the differences. Joy, laughter, and happiness are gifts from the Lord, and they breathe life into our soul. But sadness and depression are curses brought on by the enemy of our soul, Satan. Positive versus negative. Light versus darkness. They are polar extremes, and it's easy to tell the difference between them. John 10:10 (NKJV) says, "The thief does not come except to steal, and to kill, and to destroy. I have come that they may have life, and that they may have it more abundantly." Do you notice the difference between the first part of the verse and the second part of the verse? Basically, death and life are the highlights. The thief is Satan, which brings death, and Jesus is life and life more abundantly.

Jesus endured so much for us to have His joy! Hebrews 12:2 (NKJV) says, "Looking unto Jesus, the author and finisher of our faith, who for the joy that was set before Him endured the cross, despising the shame, and has sat down at the right hand of the throne of God." Jesus endured the cross…can you just see Him on that old rugged cross and His blood that was poured out for us? Jesus made the ultimate sacrifice of love. By enduring the cross, He gave us joy and life through His death! Salvation is ours, and all we have to do is turn our heart to Him by surrendering every piece of our flesh to Him. "Repent therefore and be converted, that your sins may be blotted out, so that times of refreshing may come from the presence of the Lord" (Acts 3:19, NKJV).

Have you allowed Jesus to introduce His joy to you? This kind of joy will *only* come when you lay all your burdens at the foot of the cross. Giving it *all* to Jesus and receiving the *joy* He already paid for! But life will give you a choice every day. It is up to you to decide to live a life of joy, peace, and happiness. You can also choose the opposite end of sadness, depression, and drama. I'll choose the way of Christ every time. Joy is greater and better than sadness every single time. One will bring you life; the other will bring you death. Don't get me wrong—life will hand you some very difficult times…losing a child, a parent, a job, or you may lose your home and finances. These are difficult things without a doubt. But the Bible is very clear that we are to mourn only for a moment, and then we are to move on. Psalm 30:5b (NKJV) says that "weeping may endure for a night, but joy comes in the morning." This doesn't mean that you go to bed one night after a tragedy in your life occurs and you wake up full of joy. No…the mourning/grief process is meant to be only for a season. It is not a place where we are to set up house. We visit that place for a short time, and then we work through the pain by inviting Jesus into that place of wounding. He will guide you through to a place of total healing. You don't have to repress the feelings and pretend it never happened. You acknowledge the pain, you confess it to the Lord, and you ask the Holy Spirit to lead you through the deep waters and take you to a place of total healing.

"Deep within me are these lovesick longings, desires and daydreams of living in union with you. When I'm near you, my heart and my soul will sing and worship with my joyful songs of you, my true source and spring of life!" (Psalm 84:2, TPT). Does your relationship with Jesus bring about the kind of lovesick longings described in Psalm 84? If not, seek Him out with your whole heart, dying to self and surrendering your entire spirit, soul, and body to Him. You won't regret it! Look, living a Christian life isn't easy; it's impossible without Jesus. But He is our source for all things. He is the giver of life.

I urge you to meet Him in your secret place and cry out to Him with all your heart and find this joy that can *only* come from Him! Friends, is He your true source of joy?

Jesus, You are my true source of joy. Help me seek You and find You. I want more of You and less of me. In Jesus' name. Amen.

DAY 81:

"Pray without Ceasing"

"Rejoice in our confident hope. Be patient in trouble, and keep on praying."

Romans 12:12 (NLT)

So what comes to mind for you when you read the title for today…"Pray without Ceasing"? I can only imagine the comments that would come back if this were a webpage or social media post. I would expect to hear something like…"that's impossible," "I have a job to do," "how am I supposed to pray constantly?" etc., etc. Many who identify as Christians probably don't pray for more than a few minutes a day. If we are honest with ourselves, we likely think if something needs to happen, then it's up to us to make it happen, or it must be God's will, which is not necessarily true. That's the prevailing attitude in our culture today. We look to prayer as a last resort, not the first solution.

What does it mean to pray without ceasing? This term actually was coined by the apostle Paul in 1 Thessalonians 5:17, "pray without ceasing," which is actually part of a list of exhortations for godly living in 1 Thessalonians 5:12–22. I highly encourage you to read this whole section of Scripture. Paul is not saying that we are to keep our head bowed low in a state of constant excessive talking twenty-four hours per day. He is saying that we are to be in a constant state of being aware of God's presence in our lives and to live a life surrendered to His will. Every waking moment is to be lived in an awareness that God is with us, for us, and He is actively involved in our thoughts and actions. I love this quote on prayer from one of God's great generals, Smith Wigglesworth, "I don't often spend more than half an hour in prayer at one time, but I never go more than half an hour without praying." Now that is a man of prayer! Because of this intimate, personal relationship with God, Smith Wigglesworth operated in extraordinary miracles with unusual methods.

Prayers and repentance should be part of our daily lives. Sadly, in the Western world, prayer is just something that is added into our lives wherever we can fit it in. We don't really consider it a necessary part of our life. But in the ancient world prayer was as much a part of life as the air we breathe. The beauty of prayer is that there is no method to it. God expects to hear from you just as you are; he doesn't want you faking your way through it. Prayer is meant to be a dialogue with God, not a monologue where we air out our laundry list of needs and wants. Prayer is the place where intimacy with our Heavenly Father is built. Prayer is where we commune with our true Father. He wants you to know Him…He already knows you.

But what happens when the prayer you've prayed doesn't get answered the way you expect? He answers in one of three ways…yes, no, or not now. So what should you do when God doesn't answer right away or not all? You wait. If He doesn't answer in any of those ways, perhaps you're praying for the wrong thing or praying the wrong way or praying with the wrong heart. The truth of the matter is that when things get tough, we either turn more to God in prayer or we turn away from Him entirely. There is very little room in between the two places. It can be especially tough to pray in times of sickness, the death of a loved one, or some other deeply rooted loss. The devil comes during these times to keep us from turning to our true source of strength. He aims to keep us weak and separated from God Almighty. As Christians going through our day, prayer should be our first response to every fearful situation, every anxious thought, and every undesired task that God commands. If you're unsure how to pray, start with praying the Lord's prayer every day. This is the model for us to pray…it is the way Jesus taught His disciples to pray in Matthew 6:9–13 (NKJV):

> *In this manner, therefore, pray: Our Father in heaven, Hallowed be Your name. Your kingdom come. Your will be done On earth as it is in heaven. Give us this day our daily bread. And forgive us our debts, As we forgive our debtors. And do not lead us into temptation But deliver us from the evil one. For Yours is the kingdom and the power and the glory forever. Amen.*

If you don't have a daily prayer life, I strongly encourage you to develop one. I find it very helpful to find a place where I can be alone with Him, a secret place, or a room in my home (I have a prayer closet) where I can have quiet and stillness, just Jesus and me. I would encourage you today to find your place and sit quietly with Him. Let Him speak to your heart and heal any areas that might need some healing! He is willing and would love to have that spiritual intimacy with you! I pray for complete healing of your mind, body, and soul in the mighty name of Yeshua.

This should be a natural, daily part of your life. Paul starts off in this verse to rejoice in hope. Not rejoice in results. Our hope is in Jesus Christ…He is our source for all things, but especially hope. So, during your time of loss, draw close to Him in prayer. Seek His face, not His hand. His presence is all you truly need. So let's make it personal…have you prayed today? Have you asked Jesus to forgive you of all sins in your life?

> *Jesus, I pray You teach me to be more like You. May my prayer life be so on fire for You that every mountain in my way be thrown into the sea. As I find my secret place with You and worship through the storm knowing You are enough for me. In Jesus' mighty name. Amen.*

DAY 82:

"God's Perfect Plan"

"Let joy be your continual feast. Make your life a prayer. And in the midst of everything be always giving thanks, for this is God's perfect plan for you in Christ Jesus."

1 Thessalonians 5:16–18 (TPT)

I believe every child is a gift from God. There are so many unwanted pregnancies in the world, and adoption is such a great idea. I pray that many of you reading this now who were thinking about adoption…this will be your sign and you will step out in faith and do it.

It makes me think of Moses' mother. Her name was Jochabed. A beautiful Hebrew woman who went to the extreme to save her baby. The rest of the story is quite captivating and displays the goodness of God. The story is described in the Bible in Exodus 2. Interestingly, the mother and father of Moses are not mentioned by name; they are simply described as being from the house of Levi. You may or may not know your early Hebrew history, but the house of Levi, or the Levite tribe, is known for being the priestly tribe.

The story takes place in Egypt. The Israelites are living under the heavy hand of Pharaoh. Jochabed, Moses' mother, is only mentioned by name in the Bible in Exodus 6:20 and Numbers 26:59, along with his father, Amram. These two scriptures, however, don't provide a lot of detail about Moses' parents… these scriptures simply name the parents in a genealogy of the Levites. During this very difficult time of the Israelites in Egypt, Pharaoh became very concerned about the size of the Hebrew nation even though he enslaved the Jewish nation. It says in Exodus 1:12 (NKJV), "But the more they afflicted them, the more they multiplied and grew. And they were in dread of the children of Israel." The concern over the nation of Israel became so great that Pharaoh spoke with the Hebrew midwives and ordered that every Hebrew male child be killed. But the midwives feared God and did not do as the king of Egypt ordered. Fortunately, God favored the Hebrew midwives, and they were not harmed. However, in Exodus 1:22, "Pharaoh commanded all his people, saying, 'Every son who is born you shall cast into the river, and every daughter you shall save alive.'" This is where Amram and Jochabed bore a son, Moses. Jochabed saw that Moses was a beautiful child, and she hid him for three months. She could no longer hide him, so she built an ark out of bullrushes, coated it with tar and pitch to seal it, and sent it down the Nile River, where Pharaoh's daughter had gone out to bathe. Jochabed had sent Moses' sister, Miriam, down the river to follow the ark to learn what would happen to Moses. When the daughter of Pharaoh saw the ark in the river, she sent her maid to get it. She opened the ark, and Moses began crying out, and she had compassion on the baby. She noticed that he was a Hebrew child. Miriam, who was watching the action from the sideline, yelled out to the daughter of Pharaoh and said, "Shall I go and call a nurse for you from the Hebrew women that she may nurse the child for you?" (Exodus 2:7, NKJV). Miriam went and retrieved her mother, Jochabed, to nurse her own baby. Not only did she get to nurse her own child in her home, but she was paid by Pharaoh's daughter to do it. When Moses had grown, Jochabed took her son to Pharaoh's daughter where he would be raised in the palace of Pharaoh.

Anybody who knows anything about Moses knows the rest of the story. While Moses was adopted by Pharaoh's daughter, he was still a Hebrew. To shorten the story, we can say Moses became the leader of Israel and led the Exodus out of Egypt. Moses was the author of the Torah, the Hebrew book of the law (the first five books of the Bible), which is the basis of the Jewish faith.

Sometimes adoption is the wise choice. Jochabed made a very difficult decision to allow another woman to raise her child. But in making that difficult decision, not only did Jochabed save her son, but she also saved her nation. What if you were put in a situation where the only way your baby could survive was by giving him away? Would you be able to make that decision?

Giving up your baby when circumstances dictate that you would be unable to care for your child properly is a wise decision. Nowadays, especially in the United States, abortion has become the other choice. But abortion only brings death when there are many families that are unable to have children, for whatever reason, where the baby could grow to lead a nation or maybe become a doctor who discovers a cure for cancer. The child that you may have to give up could impact the world in a way that no one else ever has. If you knew that the baby you were going to give up for adoption would change the world, would you still decide to abort the baby? But what if the baby you gave away was just a normal child who would grow up well-loved and well-cared-for? Would you make the choice to save his life or take his life through abortion?

Jesus, help me make hard decisions when they come along. I need to hear Your voice so I can obey and watch Your hand over my life and the lives of my children. In Jesus' name. Amen.

DAY 83:

"The Goodness of God"

"You're kind and tenderhearted to those who don't deserve it and very patient with people who fail you. Your love is like a flooding river overflowing its banks with kindness. God, everyone sees your goodness, for your tender love is blended into everything you do."

Psalm 145:8–9 (TPT)

Another kind of loss people never really think of is the loss or betrayal of a friend or family member. There is such a deep pain associated with this loss that only Jesus can heal it. Imagine your most trustworthy friend or family member who knows you better than anybody. They know your comings and goings, your thoughts before you even speak to them… This type of loss can be utterly devastating. All that built-up trust from years of close-knit intimacy is gone in a moment. There is a process to this loss; it's very similar to a death…it is a death, the death of the relationship the way we knew it.

In this loss the first step to obtain healing is to repent for any part you may have in the broken relationship. You repent whether you feel as though you've done anything wrong or not. The next step is to go to that person and ask for forgiveness for your part in the brokenness. Many times, if the relationship is completely severed, they won't receive that apology or offer you forgiveness. But forgiveness isn't really for them; it's a clearing of your conscience freeing you from the bondage of unforgiveness toward that person. Unforgiveness will certainly hold you in bondage, and it is a doorway that allows the evil one access to other areas of your life.

You might be asking yourself, *How do I know when I have truly forgiven someone?* First, let me start by saying that forgiveness is a process. You don't forgive someone by simply saying the words "I forgive you." You can say the words, but if your heart isn't right, then you haven't really forgiven at all. How you know your heart is good is when you hear that person's name who has betrayed you and you no longer have deep feelings of anger, sadness, or hatred toward that person. In fact, you may get to a place where you feel deep sorrow for them. When you love someone deeply and they betray you, the love for them never really goes away if your heart is good. Unforgiveness is like drinking poison and expecting the other person to die. Think of Jesus. He was betrayed by Judas. He even knew the betrayal would happen. However, Jesus still loved Judas. Jesus didn't want Judas to head down the path of destruction, but He knew there was nothing He could have said or done to change the course of events that led to His crucifixion.

Some of you may be wondering how you forgive someone who is already dead. The process is still the same whether the betrayer is alive or dead. You see, forgiveness is about your release, not theirs. You're not saying you forget about the betrayal or the wound. In fact, I say you can still remember the betrayal, but it no longer has any impact on you. Dead or alive, God expects you to forgive those who have wronged you. It really is that simple.

The fact is that we all will spend eternity in one of two destinations. This earth is not our final stop. The one who betrayed will have to answer for the betrayal. Either it will be here on this earth before death comes knocking on their door, or they will answer to it in heaven or hell. We all make mistakes. Sometimes those mistakes are big ones, and sometimes they are tiny mistakes. Sometimes we have to swallow our pride and forgive or be forgiven or both. The choice is up to us…that is what free will is all about. For me, I want to make sure I forgive quickly so no bitter root springs up in my life. How about you? Will you allow bitterness of heart to take root in you? Or will you forgive quickly and have your conscience cleared?

Jesus, help me forgive anyone who has betrayed me or anyone who feels I have betrayed them. Let only the love of You come between us and heal all our wounds. In Jesus' name.

Amen.

DAY 84:

"Not of This World"

"Jesus answered, 'My kingdom is not of this world. If My kingdom were of this world, My servants would fight, so that I should not be delivered to the Jews; but now My kingdom is not from here.'"

John 18:36 (NKJV)

Losing someone you love is very difficult. It's a heartbreak we feel like will never go away. I've heard people say time heals all wounds, but the truth is Jesus heals all wounds. I remember losing my son and wondering, *How do I go forward with this situation? Where is God in this, and why did He allow this to happen?* It took me many years to get this answer. It came when I truly turned to Him for the answer and not the world. I needed Him to tell me about heaven and where my son was. This was a revelation for me. I could just imagine my tiny son running and playing on the streets of gold and knowing he was in no more pain. His first breath on this earth only lasted a few minutes, but his next one lasted for eternity!

Let's learn some more on heaven. The Bible has many scriptures to tell us more. One of my favorites is about the mansions having many rooms.

> *Let not your heart be troubled; you believe in God, believe also in Me. In My Father's house are many mansions; if it were not so, I would have told you. I go to prepare a place for you. And if I go and prepare a place for you, I will come again and receive you to Myself; that where I am, there you may be also.*

John 14:1–3 (NKJV)

God Himself is the architect of your mansion…can you just imagine that? While we are still on this earth, God is designing every last room in your forever home.

Not only will you be getting a fabulous place to call home, but you will be where there is no sorrow, no weeping, and no sadness. If you've been raised in church, your idea of heaven may be quite different than somebody who doesn't have that background. A lot of what has been taught about heaven in our Western churches is based on a lot of religiosities. I remember, as a child, thinking heaven was sitting

203

on a big fluffy cloud along with these tiny little angels that resemble Cupid singing, "Holy, holy, holy is the Lord God Almighty." That may, in fact, be part of heaven, except for the tiny angels. But there is so much more than we could ever ask or imagine. Most Christians miss the point of heaven because of this religious mindset.

Heaven is a kingdom unto itself and is the home of the Father (see Matthew 6:9–10). "Our Father in heaven, Hallowed be Your name. Your kingdom come. Your will be done On earth as it is in heaven" (Matthew 6:9–10, NKJV). Heaven isn't some made-up place, and this earth surely isn't heaven. "Our help is in the name of the Lord, Who made heaven and earth" (Psalm 124:8, NKJV). Father God made heaven for Himself and all those who believe. "By the word of the Lord the heavens were made, And all the host of them by the breath of His mouth" (Psalm 33:6, NKJV). He spoke it into existence!

According to Jesus in Luke 15:7 (NKJV), "I say to you that likewise there will be more joy in heaven over one sinner who repents than over ninety-nine just persons who need no repentance." However, not everyone who professes His name will get to heaven as He said in Matthew 7:21 (NKJV), "Not everyone who says to Me, 'Lord, Lord,' shall enter the kingdom of heaven, but he who does the will of My Father in heaven." We can claim the blood of Jesus all we want, but if there is no transformation in our lives and we are not doing His will, then we are just a sinful person claiming the goodness of God. The apostle Paul says the old things have passed away: "Therefore, if anyone is in Christ, he is a new creation; old things have passed away; behold, all things have become new" (2 Corinthians 5:17, NKJV). And in verses 20–21 of 2 Corinthians 5, "Now then, we are ambassadors for Christ, as though God were pleading through us: we implore you on Christ's behalf, be reconciled to God. For He made Him who knew no sin to be sin for us, that we might become the righteousness of God in Him." We can't just say a little three-sentence prayer and expect that we have punched our ticket to heaven. God's Word is clear—we have a role to play, and we must die to self and seek to do His will. The prayer of repentance is only the first step.

But even heaven is not our final destination as a believer in Jesus Christ.

> *Now I saw a new heaven and a new earth, for the first heaven and the first earth had passed away. Also, there was no more sea. Then I, John, saw the holy city, New Jerusalem, coming down out of heaven from God, prepared as a bride adorned for her husband. And I heard a loud voice from heaven saying, "Behold, the tabernacle of God is with men, and He will dwell with them, and they shall be His people. God Himself will be with them and be their God. And God will wipe away every tear from their eyes; there shall be no more death, nor sorrow, nor crying. There shall be no more pain, for the former things have passed away."*

A new heaven and new earth is our final destination. It will exceed everything we know about heaven and earth. Lastly, we will get to reign with God for all eternity.

> *And he showed me a pure river of water of life, clear as crystal, proceeding from the throne of God and of the Lamb. In the middle of its street, and on either side of the river, was the tree of life, which bore twelve fruits, each tree yielding its fruit every month. The leaves of the tree were for the healing of the nations. And there shall be no more curse, but the throne of God and of the Lamb shall be in it, and His servants shall serve Him. They shall see His face, and His name shall be on their foreheads. There shall be no night there: They need no lamp nor light of the sun, for the Lord God gives them light. And they shall reign forever and ever.*

Revelation 22:1–5 (NKJV)

The end of the book says we win! Are you ready to reign for all eternity with your Father in heaven?

Jesus, heaven is a real place, and I know my loved one is safe, awaiting my return. Help me wait patiently on You and to be obedient until my name is called home. In Jesus' name. Amen.

DAY 85:

"The Price of Love"

"So you have sorrow now, but I will see you again; then you will rejoice, and no one can rob you of that joy."

John 16:22 (NLT)

I lost my pappy at the very young age of ten years old. I felt like my world had fallen apart. I loved him with everything in me. He was kind and loving to me and showed me so many little things in life, like the love of a simple daisy. He would pick daisies for me, and to this day it's my favorite flower. It was all in the simpler ways of life. When he departed to step into eternity, I had no idea how things in my life would change and how much he would be missed in my life. I named my rainbow baby his name in remembrance of him. I was and am still so proud of that old-timey Hebrew name that will run through my family line. My son has so many of his ways. I watched him with his own daughter, and I can remember me reaching up for his hand very much like my grandbaby does my son. Such a wonderful reminder of the love we shared. God has a way of giving us gentle reminders of our loved ones who have walked the path to heaven ahead of us. While we mourn the death, our loved ones who know the Lord are living in eternal bliss.

After my pappy's death, I got very close to my grandmother. I wasn't that close to her before my pappy's death, but we were drawn to each other as life continued for both of us. She was a wise beautiful soul and loved the Lord very much! She would teach me many things through the years, and most of them I thought were nonsense at the time. But now these are treasures that I hold onto, and I teach my own grandchildren the same truths she taught me. She told me once the price of love is death. It took me years to understand these words. When we love someone, and I mean truly love someone, it will always end in pain because death is a must. How often do we catch little nuggets like this over the years, never really knowing what they mean until we come face to face with the wisdom that can only be experienced and not so much learned? It's only when we experience such things that we can truly understand the meaning behind the wisdom.

I had all my children whom she got to love on and enjoy for a while until cancer took her to heaven. While death is hard and not really understood a lot, we must find comfort in His Word and in His promises. Life is a very short span of time in the view of eternity. While we make plans here on earth for

207

years on down the road, life has a way of changing everything. I love how this is talked about in James 4:14 of the Good News Translation, "You don't even know what your life tomorrow will be! You are like a puff of smoke, which appears for a moment and then disappears." That is what our lives look like when we compare our short seventy, eighty, or even ninety years to all of eternity. It's just a blip on the radar of time.

While our loved ones are no longer present on this earth…their earth bodies are no more than just an empty tent. Our spirit is where our true life resides. The spiritual bodies will live on in eternity, awaiting the day we are all together again. That's where my hope is. My hope is in Jesus Christ alone. He truly is my cornerstone and all that is good and righteous in my life. I will be reunited with my loved ones one day; in this I have much confidence because I know what the Lord says and I have experienced His truths.

There is the promise of eternity in heaven for those of us who believe that Jesus Christ is our Savior and that He died for our sins. There is nothing we can do to earn this great gift! It was the Father's lavish love to give us the life of His Son in exchange for the mess of our own lives. We give Him our sinfulness, and He gives us a pardon with eternal life in the kingdom of God. I'll take that exchange all day, every day! It's really a blood covenant. A divine exchange of His blood for ours…it's the comingling of two souls making them one. The blood of Jesus Christ seals your redemption from sin and entitles you to eternal life in a place where there are no words to describe. It's beyond your wildest imagination. It's a place of sheer perfection and no faults. It's a place of peace, love, and unity in spirit. There are no tears, no fighting, no division, no anger, or hatred. As a believer, that place is one day our new home! I am looking forward to the day I enter through those pearly gates. Do you have that promise to look forward to?

Jesus, I know this place is not my home. I am just passing by. I am excited for the day I get to see You face to face and leave behind this world because it has nothing to offer me. My reward is with You. In Jesus' name. Amen.

DAY 86:

"Messiah"

I kept looking in the night visions, And behold, on the clouds of heaven One like a Son of Man was coming, And He came up to the Ancient of Days And was presented before Him. And to Him (the Messiah) was given dominion (supreme authority), Glory and a kingdom, That all the peoples, nations, and speakers of every language Should serve and worship Him. His dominion is an everlasting dominion Which will not pass away; And His kingdom is one Which will not be destroyed.

Daniel 7:13–14 (AMP)

Do you know the Messiah? Have you met Him yet? Jesus is the Messiah. His Hebrew name is Yeshua HaMashiac. In Hebrew this name of Jesus means "anointed salvation." How's that for a family name? Most Christians only think of Jesus in terms of the New Testament. But the absolute truth is Jesus is on every page of the Bible. From Genesis chapter 1 to Revelation 22, Jesus is on every page. Even in Genesis 1:26 (NKJV), "Then God said, 'Let Us make man in Our image, according to Our likeness; let them have dominion over the fish of the sea, over the birds of the air, and over the cattle, over all the earth and over every creeping thing that creeps on the earth.'" This scripture clearly says *us*, not I. *Us* implies more than one person of God. So Jesus was from the beginning.

There are some 200 names and titles of Christ found in the Bible. I can't go into all of these names and titles in this short devotional, but I'll give you some details into some of my favorites. He is Alpha and Omega in Revelation 1:8 and 22:13. Jesus declared Himself to be the beginning and the end of all things, a reference to no one but the true God. He is referred to as Emmanuel in Isaiah 9:6 and Matthew 1:23, which means literally "God with us." Both of these scriptures affirm that the Christ who would be born in Bethlehem would be God Himself, who came to earth in the form of man to live among His people. He is "I Am" in John 8:58 and Exodus 3:14. When Jesus called Himself this title, the Jews of His day tried to stone Him for blasphemy. They understood that He was declaring Himself to be the eternal God, the unchanging Yahweh of the Old Testament. How about two distinctly different titles that seem directly opposite of one another? The Good Shepherd and the Lamb of God. The Good Shepherd title can be found in John 10:11, 14. In Bible times, a good shepherd was willing to risk his own life to protect his sheep from predators. Jesus laid down His life for His sheep, and He cares for and nurtures and feeds us. He is referred to as the Lamb of God in John 1:29; God's law called for the sacrifice of a perfect, spotless, unblemished lamb as an atonement for sin. Jesus became that Lamb.

Jehova-Rapha means "the Lord who heals" in Hebrew. Jehova-Rapha appears in Exodus 15:26 (NKJV), "If you diligently heed the voice of the Lord your God and do what is right in His sight, give ear to His commandments and keep all His statutes, I will put none of the diseases on you which I have brought on the Egyptians. For I am the Lord who heals you."

> *Jesus…showed that He was the Great Physician who heals the sick. In Galilee, Jesus went from town to town, "healing every disease and sickness among the people" (Matthew 4:23). In Judea "large crowds followed him, and he healed them there" (Matthew 19:2). In fact, "wherever he went—into villages, towns or countryside—they placed the sick in the marketplaces. They begged him to let them touch even the edge of his cloak, and all who touched it were healed" (Mark 6:56). Not only did Jesus heal people physically, He also healed them spiritually by forgiving their sins (Luke 5:20). Every day, in every way, Jesus proved Himself to be Jehovah-Rapha in the flesh.[20]*

Jehovah-Jireh means "the Lord will provide." It is the name memorialized in Genesis 22:1–8 by Abraham when God provided the ram to be sacrificed in place of Isaac.

> *As they near the site, Isaac questions Abraham concerning the intended offering: "Where is the lamb?" With great faith and foresight, Abraham responds, "God himself will provide the lamb for the burnt offering, my son" (Genesis 22:1–8). The New Testament tells us that Abraham believed God would raise Isaac from the dead (Hebrews 11:19).[21]*

Jehovah-Jireh provided a sacrifice to save Isaac, and that action was a foreshadowing of the provision of His Son for the salvation of the world.

There are many names and titles, but you can only know Him as these names/titles if you have experienced Him in those terms. If He has healed you, then you know Him as Jehovah-Rapha. If He has provided for you, then you know Him as Jehovah-Jireh. We all should know Him as the Good Shepherd as He left the ninety-nine to pursue the one…the one is you. He is pursuing you and me even to this day. What names or titles do you know your Messiah as?

> *Lord, I want to know You as my Messiah. Come walk and talk with me…lead me down the path You have for me. I love You, Lord. In Jesus' mighty name. Amen.*

---

20 "What Does It Mean That God Is Jehovah-Rapha?" Got Questions, last updated May 1, 2023, https://www.gotquestions.org/Jehovah-Rapha.html.

21 "What Does It Mean That God Is Jehovah-Jireh?" Got Questions, last updated March 1, 2022, https://www.gotquestions.org/Jehovah-Jireh.html.

DAY 87:

"The Veil"

Therefore, since we have such hope, we use great boldness of speech—unlike Moses, who put a veil over his face so that the children of Israel could not look steadily at the end of what was passing away. But their minds were blinded. For until this day the same veil remains unlifted in the reading of the Old Testament, because the veil is taken away in Christ. But even to this day, when Moses is read, a veil lies on their heart. Nevertheless, when one turns to the Lord, the veil is taken away. Now the Lord is the Spirit; and where the Spirit of the Lord is, there is liberty.

2 Corinthians 3:12–17 (NKJV)

Friends, my heart has been heavy for the lost souls. I have family and friends who are unsaved or think since they said a prayer at ten years old, they are saved. Once saved, always saved…well, what's our fruit look like? Has there been any change in your life after you gave your life to Jesus Christ? Galatians 5:22–23 explains what we should look like. The time is ripe for bringing the lost and unbelieving to Christ. We have revival breaking out all over the world, even here in the United States. People are hungry for the truth!

The problem is that most of our lost loved ones and unbelieving friends have a veil, as it were, over their heart, and their eyes are blinded by the enemy. The apostle Paul describes this perfectly in the book of 2 Corinthians in today's passage noted above. The "veils" separate us from seeing Jesus clearly, and He is more than able to take those veils away.

Although Paul was speaking of the Jews in this passage, the "veils" easily apply to us today. Paul goes on to further explain the veil in 2 Corinthians 4:3–6. Expanding the dilemma and the hope to all unbelievers.

But even if our gospel is veiled, it is veiled to those who are perishing, whose minds the god of this age has blinded, who do not believe, lest the light of the gospel of the glory of Christ, who is the image of God, should shine on them. For it is the God who commanded light to shine out of darkness, who has shone in our hearts to give the light of the knowledge of the glory of God in the face of Jesus Christ.

2 Corinthians 4:3–6 (NKJV)

These verses give us a backdrop of how we should pray for the unbelieving people in our lives. Prayer is essential in evangelism. It is more important to talk to God about men than to talk to men about God. Both of these works are important, but God wants to hear from us on our perspective regarding those we view as lost. The truth is God views no one as beyond His grasp until their last breath. After that their decision to reject Christ is final. But until that moment, all things are possible through Christ.

In the Bible, there are common functions of veils, covering, consecration, and separation. In the Old Testament, when Moses descended Mount Sinai with the Ten Commandments, the skin of his face shone because he had been talking with God (see Exodus 34:29–35). The people were extremely afraid when they saw the glory of the Lord on Moses' face. So Moses had to veil his face to keep the people from seeing the glory that was radiating from his face. Moses' veil concealed the light of God's glory from the people.

Exodus 26:31–34 features the veil placed in the tabernacle. This veil was an ornate, thick curtain that hung as a wall of separation between the holy place and the most holy place, or the holy of holies, where the ark of the testimony and mercy seat were placed. Only the high priest could enter this place once a year to offer a sacrifice for the sins of the people. It was in this place that God promised to dwell among His people (Exodus 30:6).

In Matthew 17:2 (NKJV), Jesus' glory was unveiled for the three chosen disciples, James, John, and Peter, to see the fullness of His majesty and glory shining along with Moses and Elijah. His face shone on the earth as "the radiance of the glory of God and the exact imprint of His nature." I love how The Passion Translation describes the glory of Jesus… "The Son is the dazzling radiance of God's splendor, the exact expression of God's true nature—His mirror image!" (Hebrews 1:3). The "unveiled face" speaks of a mind uncovered, not blinded but fully revealed glorious majesty of Jesus Christ, which requires divine revelation.

At the moment of Jesus' atoning death on the cross, "the veil…was torn in two from top to bottom" (Matthew 27:51, NKJV). And this was nothing like the curtains or shears we place on our windows today. This veil was thirty feet high and wide, as thick as a man's hand. No man could tear that veil! Only God! According to Hebrews 10:19–22, Jesus' flesh is that torn veil. Jesus, acting as high priest, entered the most holy place on our behalf, placing His own blood on the mercy seat, securing our eternal redemption and giving us access directly to God.

Jesus made a way when there seemed to be no way. Jesus is our eternal sacrifice that was made on behalf of each one of us, thus creating the new blood covenant. It is through this blood covenant that God made the way for eternal redemption through His Son, Jesus Christ. This is why we can say Jesus is the way, the truth, and the life (John 14:6). Jesus was fully God, and He walked this earth as fully man, denying His sovereignty, living in humility in flesh, fulfilling every prophecy in Scripture. He truly is the only way to the Father in heaven. Have you made Jesus your way?

Merciful God, God of our salvation, I pray that Your Spirit would burn away every veil and every blinder over the heart and mind of [who I'm praying for]. Let every veil and every blinder the Enemy has placed over their heart and mind be utterly removed, so that they may see the glory of God in the face of Jesus. Jesus, I pray You would reveal Yourself to them, Lord. Walk into their lives. Make Yourself known! May they see You, encounter You, and receive You. Let the light of God shine in their heart to give them the knowledge of God in the face of Christ. In Jesus' name I pray![22]

---

22 "Praying for Those Who Don't Believe," Wild at Heart, posted April 10, 2023, https://wildatheart.org/blogs/john/praying-those-who-dont-believe.

DAY 88:

"The Potter's Clay"

"After you have suffered for a little while, the God of all grace [who imparts His blessing and favor], who called you to His own eternal glory in Christ, will Himself complete, confirm, strengthen, and establish you [making you what you ought to be]."

1 Peter 5:10 (AMP)

When I think of the words at the end of this verse, "making you what you ought to be," it draws me to a vision of a potter working in clay. There's something beautiful about the way a potter works. They take a lump of unformed clay and skillfully shape it on the potter's wheel with pressure in just the right places. This does a couple of things to the clay; first, it removes any imperfections hidden in the clay, and it also creates the desired shape matching the vision of the final piece in the potter's mind.

The loss of a child creates a massive amount of pressure on a family, especially upon the mother. While the father of the child also deals with tremendous stress and pressure, it's a different form of pressure and stress than what the mother often endures. While Daddy will be concerned about the loss and will mourn that loss, he is also tasked with returning his home to a state of "normality." How do you get on with the business of life after losing a child? The world is not sympathetic to your loss…sad but true nonetheless. Bills will mount up. Work will beckon. Family and friends, while attempting to empathize, will urge you to get back to "normal." A lot of this return to normality falls on Daddy. He hasn't even had the time to obtain healing from this deep place of hurt before he must return to life.

However, Mommy must also deal with the return to normal, but she also must deal with an empty nursery, her body that is still responding to the aftereffects of having a child, and likely a deep depression that hangs over her like a cloud. Mommy deals with many different emotions, pressure, and stress.

Both Mommy and Daddy must deal with the condition of their own soul before they are ever able to heal. Or before they can return to a place where they can even have a normal conversation without the subject of their loss being brought up.

The pressure created by the loss of a child will be used by the Father to remove the hidden imperfections within us. This pressure will also shape our character to match the vision of the Master Creator in heaven. Your suffering has a purpose. I am reminded of Romans 5:3–5 (NIV), which says:

Not only so, but we also glory in our sufferings, because we know that suffering produces perseverance; perseverance, character; and character, hope. And hope does not put us to shame, because God's love has been poured out into our hearts through the Holy Spirit, who has been given to us.

This piece of Scripture is all about peace and hope.

But this passage in Romans also brings us back to our verse today from 1 Peter 5. Those words, after you have suffered a little while, are not words anyone wants to hear. The suffering comes with a promise. After you have suffered a while, Jesus Himself will perfect, establish, strengthen, and settle you (see verse 10 in the NKJV). Suffering is never present, and nobody wants to endure it! But with the promise of Jesus perfecting you…would that make the suffering worth it? I'm not certain this is a question anyone can answer until they are on the other side of the suffering.

The question remains—are you willing to endure the suffering to be perfected, established, strengthened, and settled by Jesus Christ?

Jesus, I am so grateful my name is written in Your book and that You knew me before I was formed in my mother's womb. You formed and molded me into what You wanted me to be. Help me to be more and more like You, Father. In Jesus' name. Amen.

DAY 89:

"The Shelter of His Wing"

I am standing in absolute stillness, silent before the one I love, waiting as long as it takes for him to rescue me. Only God is my Savior, and he will not fail me. For he alone is my safe place. His wraparound presence always protects me as my champion defender. There's no risk of failure with God! So why would I let worry paralyze me, even when troubles multiply around me?

Psalm 62:5–6 (TPT)

As we are nearing the end of these ninety days of devotions, my hope and prayer for you is that you are finding Jesus as your safe place, as your defender, and the rescuer of your soul. I especially love how Hebrews 13:5b-6 (NKJV) says, "For He Himself has said, 'I will never leave you nor forsake you.' So we may boldly say: 'The Lord is my helper; I will not fear. What can man do to me?'" What peace and hope there is when you can view your circumstances through rose-colored glasses…the rose of Sharon? Jesus Christ is the healer of our soul… It sure is comforting to me to know that He is always with me even when I can't feel His presence.

Through my walk with Him, I have come to learn that my feelings will lie to me. I'm not always going to feel great about things at first, but it might work out great for me. I may not always feel poorly about something, but it could turn in my favor. My point is just as I said before…your feelings will lie to you. If God said that He would never leave us nor forsake us, why should we doubt Him? If this is you and you are doubting His goodness toward you, then change your perspective on how you are looking at God.

You need to enter His presence in your secret place and find Him where He is. Cry out to God. It's okay for you to be angry at Him, to be disappointed in Him, or to blame Him. God can take you from that place and lead you to a place of healing and to His great love. Your perspective of Him will shift as you spend more and more time in the secret place. He is a good, good Father, and He loves you with an everlasting love. He wants you to know that you are accepted and approved, you are loved, you are cared for, and you will find your peace and healing in Him. Enter into His kingdom realm…enter into His presence. He is waiting for you!

I found healing and His great love when I began to spend time with Him. My love for Him grew deeper and deeper as the days turned to months and the months turned to years. All my hurts and wounds faded in light of His presence. His glory causes all things to fade. His glory is the greatest place anywhere…there is nowhere else I'd rather be. All gloominess and darkness are gone in His presence. There is love, joy, and peace in Him. Crawl up into the lap of your Father, and everything else begins to fade away. There is no greater love than His love for you. Come boldly to the throne of grace; come into the presence of God Almighty. What do you need Him to heal in you today?

Abba, my heart is on You. I need You to walk me through this process of healing and to renew my soul. My soul is bruised and crushed; it can only heal with You. One touch from You and everything will come into alignment with Your will for my life. Thank You for loving me so deeply and for coming for me. In Jesus' name. Amen.

DAY 90:

"The Goal"

"This is why we work hard and continue to struggle, for our hope is in the living God, who is the Savior of all people and particularly of all believers."

1 Timothy 4:10 (NLT)

This has been such a beautiful journey together, and I am kind of sorry to see it end. I wanted to wait to write this last entry until I got to the beach…so here I am at one of my favorite places in the world: St. Simons Island, Georgia. There's something special about this place. You can just feel the presence of God here, but I wasn't sure why. As we wondered about the island, we ran into the cutest little chapel by the sea. We had no idea what we were about to encounter. We decided to stop by this little chapel in hopes of meeting the Holy Spirit in a new and beautiful way. His presence was all around us as we kneeled to pray. Oh, how He comes for His children.

We left the chapel to look around the grounds, which were landscaped and manicured in such an immaculate way. There were these huge centuries-old live oak trees that resembled what I could imagine the olive trees must have looked like in Israel. We saw a large statue of Jesus that stood about eight feet tall carved out of all white marble in another area that had beautiful flowers and bushes all around it. We began to walk over to it when I heard the Holy Spirit say, "It's much like the Garden of Gethsemane." I said, "Lord, there were no flowers there." He gently said, "It was a beautiful place, Jean." I thought to myself, *How could that garden be beautiful when it was a place of great agony for Him?* It was the place where He endured so much stress and pain that He sweat blood.

As I walked in and looked at the large statue of Christ with His arms open to me…I heard the words, "Come to me, all of you who are weary and burdened, and I will give you rest" (Matthew 11:28, CSB). Immediately, I knew it was the Lord. I laid my hands on His feet and just started weeping. My heart was broken for the sins I had committed before receiving Him as my sweet Savior. The pain that He endured was overwhelming to me, and I am not much of a weeper, but the tears just kept flowing as we lingered near the garden. I was trying to take in all that had just happened to me. I walked around the grounds of this chapel, and I read a marker that said, "YOU ARE STANDING ON HOLY GROUND." We didn't yet know the history of this place, but we definitely stood in agreement that the ground upon which this place was built was indeed *holy*.

219

We returned back to where we were staying, and the Spirit was still heavy upon us. Because I had mentioned the Garden of Gethsemane and what I had experienced in these gardens, my husband did a little research on the Garden of Gethsemane and found out that it was indeed a beautiful place filled with a variety of flowers at the base of an olive tree grove. The name Gethsemane means a place of prayer and weeping. This newfound information suddenly validated everything I had experienced as I walked to this beautiful little garden with a statue of Jesus.

I was wondering who built that chapel and why the Spirit was so strong there. My husband simply said, "I don't know who built it, but I keep hearing the name 'Charles.'" I started doing a little research on this land and this chapel, and as we came to find out, Charles and John Wesley founded this place and lived here for a while. There are no coincidences with the Lord! For those that may not know, Charles and John Wesley were two of the great generals for the Lord. These two men led a revival in England that transformed the entire country, and they were instrumental in a movement known as Methodism, which would later become the foundation for the Methodist Church led by John Wesley. The two brothers arrived on Georgian soil in early 1736. They sought to carry the gospel to a new land knowing they would encounter hardships that would strengthen their faith.

The end goal as a Christian is to find God in the details of your everyday life, no matter how mundane you may think it is. We didn't really intend to set out on some spiritual expedition to find a holy place to write this devotional. But God knew the ocean is a place where I especially connect with Him and feel His presence ever so clearly. So He sent me to the beach, not wanting me to write this final entry until we arrived. We looked at several different beaches, but we were strongly drawn to come back to St. Simons Island. Once we arrived, He directed our path to all the places we needed to go. My advice to you is to allow God into the tiny little moments of your day and watch how He redirects your path. He will put you exactly where you need to be exactly when you need to be there. You may need healing from your losses, or you may just want more of Him. Whatever it is you need, God will be in the middle of it designing your life and directing your path. But you have to know Him in order to receive His revelation. I have said it in numerous ways all throughout this devotional: you will find Him when you seek Him with your whole heart (see Jeremiah 29:13). Get in the Word of God and stay in the Word of God. Seek His face, and not His hand, in prayer.

We hope and pray for each one reading this book that you have found some measure of healing for your soul. Loss is a painful thing, but healing and strength are always found on the other side of brokenness. Psalm 147:3 (NKJV), "He heals the brokenhearted and binds up their wounds." Has God healed your broken heart and bound your wounds?

Jesus, I am so grateful for You and what You endured that day in the Garden of Gethsemane. As I walk through my loss, I will remember no matter what I've ever had to endure, I did not have to sweat blood. Thank You for loving me enough to die for me. In Jesus' name. Amen.

ABOUT THE AUTHOR

Jean is a faithful follower of Jesus Christ with an extreme love of Scripture and the study thereof. She is a devoted wife, mother to five wonderful sons and three angel babies with several daughters-in-law, and a mawmaw to seven beautiful and much-loved grandchildren and two boxers named Malachi and Queen Esther.

She has devoted her life, obediently, to the call of God to start and run Angels in Waiting 91:4 non-profit ministry. She gives all the glory to her Heavenly Father, Jesus Christ! Her desire is for this ministry to be nameless and faceless.

Please visit www.angelsinwaiting914.com to learn more about the ministry.

Her background is in dentistry, which was her passion for many years prior to starting Angels in Waiting 91:4.

Jean lives in Braselton, Georgia, with her husband and most of her family around her.

She is an active part of a local church and attends KINEO Ministry Training Center for further education.

Jean's first book, *The Father Gives & Takes Away: The Journey Home*, was all about the stories that come through Angels in Waiting 91:4. This power-packed short read will move you to tears, cause you to laugh, and be grateful for those God has entrusted to your care. It is a story of life after loss and was the inspiration to help mommies and daddies who have lost a baby to get on that journey home. If you haven't read that book, I encourage you to pick it up and learn more about Angels in Waiting 91:4 and discover why we do what we do. *The Father Gives & Takes Away* is very much the precursor to this devotional.

Jean wanted to offer families who have experienced loss something that could lead them into the healing arms of Jesus Christ. What better way to do that than to create a ninety-day devotional to keep you in the Word of God and provide inspiration on a daily basis?

Jean has a heart and great love for people, and she hates to see people hurting. This book, and the one written previous to this one, is her way of giving back to those experiencing great pain from losing a child. Because she has experienced this pain herself, there is no one more acquainted with healing after loss. She has dedicated her life and ministry to helping others find the healing journey home.

9 798893 331653